Until We Are Free

BY SHIRIN EBADI

◆

Until We Are Free

The Golden Cage

Iran Awakening

Until We Are Free

UNTIL WE ARE FREE

My Fight for Human Rights in Iran

SHIRIN EBADI

LONDON · SYDNEY · AUCKLAND · JOHANNESBURG

1 3 5 7 9 10 8 6 4 2

Rider, an imprint of Ebury Publishing,
20 Vauxhall Bridge Road,
London SW1V 2SA

Rider is part of the Penguin Random House group of companies
whose addresses can be found at global.penguinrandomhouse.com

Penguin
Random House
UK

First published by Rider in 2016

Published in the United States by Random House, an
imprint and division of Penguin Random House LLC,
New York in 2016

www.eburypublishing.co.uk

Grateful acknowledgement is made to Sara Khalili for permission
to reprint an extract from the poem "My Country, I Shall Build
You Again" by Simin Behbahani, translated by Sara Khalili.
Translation © Sara Khalili

A CIP catalogue record for this book is available from the British Library

Hardback ISBN 9781846045004
Trade Paperback 9781846045011

Printed and bound in Great Britain by Clays LTD, St Ives PLC

And the wrongdoers will soon know
to what place of return they shall return.

—The Holy Koran 26:227

I know how men in exile feed on dreams.

—Aeschylus

CONTENTS

◆

Death Threat

♦

I was restless. The evening was like any other, dinner at my brother's house, but I felt an anxiety I could not identify. The room was stuffy, the lamps too bright, the children louder than usual. I stepped onto the balcony for some fresh air and watched clouds darken the sky. There was a loud crack; then the rain Tehran so badly needed began to wash the toxic smog out of the air. Though it was April, and the wind should have cleared the winter pollution, I had been having a hard time breathing outside. A government official had recently said that living in a city with such poisonous air was akin to "mass suicide."

For weeks now, I had been working on a report about the government's executions of children. Every other nation on earth had stopped routinely executing minors, but Iran regularly imposed the death penalty on children for a range of crimes, from murder to manslaughter in self-defense. In 2004, the authorities sentenced a sixteen-year-old girl to death for premarital sex, or "crimes against chastity." The judge himself reputedly acted as executioner, leading the schoolgirl to the noose, blindfolding her, and motioning for the crane to hoist her from the ground. Her body hung from the crane for nearly an hour, her black chador swaying in the breeze. The state didn't want any attention brought to these executions, especially internationally, but my colleagues and I had worked hard to show a pattern of such sentencing. It was perhaps the boldest report we had ever produced, and we were due to share it with the United Nations, where we knew the Islamic Republic would face condemnation. It was that, I told myself, that was making me uneasy. If I could be back at home with a cup of tea, the report in my hand, reviewing the language and checking the details, my mind would settle.

I decided to head home early, and said goodbye to my brother and his family. The streets were mostly empty and the air smelled of exhaust and rotten leaves and rainwater as I climbed into my car. Pulling away from the curb, I noticed a mural on the side of a building, shining under a streetlamp, baiting America and the West: "Sanction us; we'll cope."

The roads were silent except for the rain under my tires. I turned onto my street, a quiet lane. No one was out in the downpour, and the sidewalk felt even more isolated than usual. My husband, Javad, was not at home, and our windows were dark. I thought about the report waiting inside, on my desk, and its horrible depictions of children hanging from cranes. I fingered the keys in my pocket anxiously. Minding the puddles, and looking nervously over my shoulder, I didn't see the note until it was directly before me. There, thumbtacked to my front door, was a message on white paper from someone who had been watching me:

If you go on as you are now, we will be forced to end your life. If you value it, stop slandering the Islamic Republic. Stop all this noise you are making outside the country. Killing you is the easiest thing we could do.

Until We Are Free

CHAPTER 1

Intimidation

◆

The story of Iran is the story of my life. Sometimes I wonder why I am so attached to my country, why the outline of Tehran's Alborz Mountains is as intimate and precious to me as the curve of my daughter's face, and why I feel a duty to my nation that overwhelms everything else. I remember when so many of my friends and relatives began leaving the country in the 1980s, disheartened by the bombs raining down from the war with Iraq and by the morality police checkpoints set up by the still new Islamic government. While I did not judge anyone for wanting to leave, I could not fathom the impulse. Did one leave the city where one's children had been born? Did one walk away from the trees in the garden one planted each year, even before they bore pomegranates and walnuts and scented apples?

For me, this was unthinkable. When I walked into

the country's highest court and the new revolutionary authorities told me that women could no longer be judges, I stayed. I stayed when the authorities demoted me to clerk in the same court I had presided over as a judge. I shut my ears when the revolutionaries who had taken over the justice system talked in my presence about how women were fickle and indecisive and unfit to mete out justice, which would now be the work of men. I stayed as the Iraqi warplanes bombed houses on our street to rubble. I stayed when the new authorities said Islam demanded violent justice, that Islam allowed for young men and women to be executed on rooftops and hung from cranes for their political beliefs, their bodies dumped in mass graves.

In the same way that I did not leave Iran, I did not leave Islam, either. If we all packed our suitcases and boarded planes, what would be left of our country? If we bowed our heads and stayed quietly at home, permitting them to say that Islam allowed the assassination of writers and the execution of teenagers, what would be left of our faith?

I wrote long letters to friends who had emigrated, on the thin, diaphanous paper we used for airmail in those days, and told them that I was still managing to live. In the mid-1980s, I stopped working altogether and turned inward, disconnected from the brutal politics of the new regime. Despite the bombs and the morality checkpoints, my husband and I raised our two girls, who went to school in pigtails and learned how to read. We had dinner together every night. My husband,

Javad, continued with his work as an engineer, and I raised the girls, contemplating how I could reinvent myself, now that the judiciary had become the realm of men.

In the early 1990s, after the war had ended, the girls were older and didn't need me as much. I briefly tried practicing family law, but I saw quickly that the courts under the Islamic Republic operated very differently than they had under the shah. The authorities permitted women to work as lawyers, but the system and all its new procedures were so dysfunctional that it was impossible to take a case forward. On several occasions, I had trouble simply trying to review a file at the courthouse. The clerk, upon realizing that I wasn't going to "tip" him for retrieving the file (corrupt countries have endless euphemisms for bribery), would say, "Sorry, the file is missing. Come back tomorrow." I would go back the next day, and he would say, "Sorry, I haven't had a chance to search for your file." On the third or fourth day, knowing that I would keep coming back, he would finally produce the file. But because I wasn't prepared to pay a bribe, I had lost two or three days of work.

It was much worse in the courts. There, the person who was willing to pay more was in the right; justice was bought, not fought for or deliberated. To protest, I eventually hung a big sign in front of my law office: "Due to the current inhospitable circumstance of the courts, I will no longer be accepting clients and can only offer legal advice." This did not feel, at the time, like a particularly risky thing to do. I was simply being honest about the country's legal climate, rather than consciously trying to defy the state. But I see now, and learned with time, how peaceful disobedience can be a powerful act of defiance. After a while, people who could not afford to hire a lawyer—often defendants who had been accused of political crimes—found their way to me.

The state of criminal law was especially grave after the 1979 revolution. The Islamic Republic had replaced the secular criminal code Iran had followed under the shah with a system of Islamic law based on seventh-century readings of sharia, Islamic law. I still vividly remember the case that revealed to me the full extent of the system's dysfunction and cruelty.

My friend Shahla Sherkat, the country's foremost feminist editor and publisher, called to ask if I could offer any advice to the family of an eleven-year-old girl named Leila. One day, as Leila was picking wildflowers in the hills outside her village, three men snuck up and attacked her. The men raped her, struck her repeatedly on the head, and then threw her to her death over a nearby cliff. The local police arrested the men. One mysteriously hung himself in prison, and the court found the other two guilty of rape and murder. Because the laws at the time valued the life of a man convicted of murder more than that of a girl raped and tossed off a cliff, Leila's family was held responsible for paying for their executions. The family was unable to come up with the money, and the men were released.

The Islamic Republic claimed that these laws were based on the principles of blood money in Islamic sharia, but I believed that not only were they unjust, they were a distortion of true Islamic legal principles.

In the course of seeking justice through the courts, Leila's family became destitute. Her mother had taken to sitting outside the courthouse each day in a white shroud, silently holding up a placard that described what had happened to her daughter. As I recounted more fully in *Iran Awakening,* I took on their case, and while I did not manage to secure anything like justice, their ordeal shaped the sort of legal response that became my second career. Though the judge in Leila's case accused me of contravening Islam in my arguments, I drew on Islamic law and principles to challenge him. I discovered that many judges in the Islamic Republic had little or no understanding of Islamic legal tenets, and also that many Iranian women had no idea of how egregiously the law discriminated against them. It was only when life dragged them to some dark crossroads—divorce, the death of a child, a fight over inheritance—that they realized how little status they had before the law.

I made a showcase out of Leila's case, writing articles and speaking out publicly, and extensive coverage in the Iranian press soon led to a public outcry. In one article I described how the criminal code around blood money holds that if a man suffers an injury that damages his testicles, he receives compensation equal to a woman's life. I posed the question this way: If a woman with a PhD is run over by a car and dies, and an illiterate thug gets his testicle hurt in a fight, the value of that woman's life and that thug's testicle are equal. Is this, I wrote, how the Islamic Republic regards its women?

For the first time since the revolution, the question of women's equality before the law came into the national spotlight. I saw then how sympathetic Iranian society was to such injustice and how powerful public outrage could be; more than anything else, it made the authorities pay attention. It was then that I started on the course that I follow to this day, seeking justice in the law through upholding the rights of those most vulnerable—women, children, dissidents, and minorities—and pushing for legal change on the battlefield of public sentiment.

The Islamic Republic has a myriad of shortcomings. It vests absolute power in an unelected supreme leader, harasses independent-minded clerics who challenge the religious basis of its severe Islamic rule, and pursues policies that are ideologically radical and detached from the national interests of the Iranian people. But like any regime committed to perpetuating its own power, it has on some occasions shown sensitivity to the condemnation of the international community and the brewing discontent of its own citizens. It is the system we have in place, and especially in those years, the 1990s and early 2000s, it made several reluctant adjustments to some of its most inhumane laws and policies, in response to the activism I and many colleagues

in the field of human rights and the women's movement pursued. This course seemed the only path possible to follow, bar packing up and leaving. Although,
in this era, Iranians began emigrating by the thousands, both those who left and those who stayed behind
remained fiercely proud of Iran the nation. We had
been ruled by autocrats, kings, and now clerics; our
history reached back thousands of years, all the way to
Cyrus the Great, the Persian king who inscribed civili-
zation's first human rights charter on a clay cylinder. I
viewed myself as an inheritor of this history, of the
great tradition of epic Persian poetry that I had read to
my girls every night before bedtime. Like most Iranians, I was bitterly disappointed in Iran's present precisely because of the love and admiration I had for its
past.

I received the Nobel Peace Prize in October 2003 for
my efforts for democracy and human rights, and
though you would think that this would have propelled
my work in Iran and won me some grudging respect, it
put me under even more pressure and scrutiny by the
government. The Iranian state did everything it could
to suppress the news of my award, forbidding the state
radio and TV stations to so much as mention it and
putting me under an even more severe news embargo.
When a reporter asked President Mohammad Khatami,
a reformist who was in power at the time, why he had

not congratulated me, he responded, "This isn't such an important prize. It's only the Nobel in literature that really matters."

But as is always the case with Iran, there are ways to get around official censorship. News that matters finds its way to those who need to hear about it. I invited a Kurdish music group to perform at the Nobel awards ceremony. The Iranian regime has discriminated against its Kurdish minority for years, denying them the right to study in their own language and to maintain their Kurdish identity in public life. Iranian Kurds across the country watched this Kurdish group performing on satellite television and wept with pride at their inclusion. It was a small act, but symbolic, and the rumor spread among Iranian Kurds that I must be of Kurdish background. While the Iranian government sought to ignore my Nobel Prize—which ultimately recognized the work of human rights defenders trying to peacefully moderate the country from within—we had reached an age when satellite television and digital media meant it was no longer possible to keep a nation in the dark.

Others took notice of the prize as well, particularly the women of Iran, who had long been working for equal rights and recognition; they saw in the Nobel committee's decision a global support and awareness of their struggle. The chancellor of the all-female Alzahra University, Zahra Rahnavard, invited me to give a public

lecture on women's legal status. Rahnavard, the first
woman to head a university since the Islamic Revolution, was a distinguished scholar and activist. The
world would come to know her in 2009, when she appeared on the front pages of newspapers as the wife of
Mir Hossein Mousavi, the Green Movement opposition leader. That day in 2003, Rahnavard greeted me
at the campus lecture theater, a tall building of yellow
brick surrounded by wide lawns dotted with young
women reading under sycamore trees. Hundreds of
students were lining up outside for seats, though the
room was already filled to capacity and buzzing with
voices. We were discussing where to put the lectern
when the doors at the back of the auditorium flew open
and a mob of about thirty women, their heads covered
by black chadors, poured in, shouting angrily.

"If Ebadi lectures here today, then tomorrow you're
going to ask for George Bush!" they yelled, pushing
toward the stage, which Rahnavard and I were standing
in front of. They were clearly not students; they were
vigilantes supported by the state. "This lecture is canceled!" they shouted. The students in the front rose
and moved toward me, forming a protective ring.
Rahnavard walked forward a few paces, her face etched
with fury.

"This lecture is being held with the official permission of the university. You have no right to disrupt it,"
she said. "All of you must leave immediately."

One of the mob women sprang forward and reached
for Rahnavard's chador. "You don't even deserve to

have this chador on your head," she said, pulling violently at the fabric, which was pinned to Rahnavard's manteau beneath.

The rest of her accomplices surged forward. The small band of students who had formed a circle around me started moving toward the back of the lecture hall. "Khanoum Ebadi," they urged, "we have got to get you out of here—follow us." They herded the chancellor and me out a back door and down a long corridor. The students led us into a small classroom and closed the door and barricaded it with chairs and tables. Soon we heard shouts and running, cries of "They're here, they're hiding in this room!" and then fists pounding against the door, trying to push it open. Rahnavard called the security services on her mobile phone.

"They've forced me to do something I never wanted to see happen. I don't believe that police should set foot on university grounds, but there's no other choice," she said to me.

The police arrived and forcibly escorted the mob of women away. We agreed that canceling the lecture seemed the safest course, and I thanked the chancellor and her colleagues for the invitation and their quick wits as we'd faced attack. We shook hands warmly, and then two officers who had stayed behind walked me safely off university grounds. Nothing ever came of the incident, the authorities made no arrests, and we never found out exactly who had dispatched the women to disrupt my lecture that day. Rahnavard threatened to resign if the authorities didn't find and prosecute those responsible. But they never did, and after Mahmoud Ahmadinejad's election, she eventually stepped down herself or was fired—it was never clear. Though discussing women's rights in Iran had always been fraught with difficulty, what happened there that day seemed the beginning of an altogether new kind of harassment and intimidation.

CHAPTER 2

A Wedding

♦

Although the Nobel Prize irritated the Iranian government, the money that accompanied it helped my work considerably. I purchased an apartment that would serve as the headquarters for the Defenders of Human Rights Center, the organization I had founded to bring numerous lawyers inside the country together to defend political prisoners and to promote the legal and human rights of Iranian citizens. The center was the most effective force challenging the Iranian government's political repression; it also functioned as a legal aid network for dissidents and victims of state repression. The Nobel money meant we could pursue more ambitious plans and programs than ever before.

I also deposited some of the money in a high-interest bank account in Iran and distributed the interest income among the families of political prisoners who were living with one breadwinner in prison and badly needed help. I put a small amount, as well, in a bank account in France to help support my daughters' studies. Since the Islamic authorities had stripped me of my judgeship in 1980, I had not been able to earn income and save money for their education, and the legal work I began to undertake in the 1990s, defending children's and women's rights, was almost entirely pro bono.

We weren't simply providing this pro bono defense because as lawyers we felt it was the right thing to do. We also had a higher goal: we wanted to help give people the courage to express their opinions. We wanted to assure them that if they were arrested because of their pro-democracy activities or for speaking their minds about citizens' rights or some other sensitive issue, they would know they'd have access to a group of lawyers who would defend them without asking for a fee and would help look after their families. We had a team of psychiatrists and medical doctors, for example, that offered free treatment to our clients' relatives.

The reports we compiled every three months were the other key effort in our work. We dedicated a great deal of time and care to them and included only abuses that were documented and verified, such as cases of arbitrary detention and harassment of activists. They were the first reports of this kind to be published inside Iran by an Iranian organization, and they soon became a staple resource for the United Nations and other international human rights groups, prompting the authorities to scrutinize the center's activities even more aggressively. We held training courses for those whose background or activities made them particularly vulnerable to arrest—student activists, religious and ethnic minorities, and journalists. We taught them about their rights should they be detained, and how to navigate the judicial process in order to secure furloughs and, sometimes, early release.

We had started the center with no expectation of ever really making a living, and we had struggled to put even a basic infrastructure in place: an office, some desks, phones that worked, a place people could come to bring their broken lives. Now, with the Nobel Prize money, the center's lawyers finally had a place to gather and work.

The same year I won the Nobel, a little-known figure was appointed mayor of Tehran. Most Iranians and, indeed, most Tehranis had not previously heard of Mahmoud Ahmadinejad, the civil engineer from working-class south Tehran. The municipal elections had drawn perhaps the poorest turnout in the city's history. Only 12 percent of the city's inhabitants voted, nearly all of them from the traditional, radical minority in society loyal to the Islamic regime. Most Iranians, disappointed by President Mohammad Khatami's failure to push forward his reforms, sat out the election. With the moderate majority absent, the conservatives easily swept the election, and the city council, composed of traditionalists and hard-liners, chose Ahmadinejad to run Tehran.

What happened next astonished everyone, especially people like me, Muslim Iranians who were quietly faithful in their personal lives but felt that religion should be a private matter, not used for extravagant political gestures. Ahmadinejad declared that the martyrs of the Iran-Iraq War deserved greater public commemoration, and he ordered that newly found remains of the war dead would be buried in seventy-two of the capital's parks and squares. The Tehran where I had spent my youth as a college student, including the parks where my husband and I had walked hand in hand during our courtship and where I had taken my girls to play when they were small, was going to be transformed into a haphazard cemetery.

Young Iranians, especially, were indignant. The city's green parks provided the few spaces where friends and couples could go to spend their free time, and given the state's strict social codes—the ban on Western films and music, the filtering of the Internet, and frequent raids on coffee shops—the parks were particularly precious. But Ahmadinejad was determined. He sent flag-draped coffins bearing veterans' remains even into Tehran's universities, and clashes erupted between furious students and the police and municipal undertakers. The biggest confrontation took place at the elite Sharif University of Technology, a feeder school for Stanford University and other top institutions in the West. Iranian universities, like universities in much of the world, are hotbeds for political activism. The students knew that the burials were intended to send a pointed message to them: that freedom of thought, education, and the physical space of the university itself belonged to the revolution and its martyrs.

Slowly Tehran became the canvas on which Ahmadinejad expressed his radical vision for the state. One afternoon, while driving, I looked up to see an enormous mural on the side of a building. It was a female Palestinian suicide bomber clutching a rifle in one hand and her little son in the other. This, it seemed, was the state's only vision of gender equality. Ahmadinejad instituted separate elevators for men and women in government buildings, and he fired swaths of municipal workers who were not religious or devoted enough to his ideology.

Tehran had long ago started to transform, beginning with the 1979 revolution itself. But the extraordinary way in which Ahmadinejad was taking charge of the city, remaking it to fit his extremist view of the world, filled me with sadness. I recalled the cosmopolitan Tehran of the 1970s in which Javad and I had courted. The elegant restaurants and manicured gardens may have reflected class inequality, but they also symbolized the aspirations of most of the city's inhabitants to lead comfortable, urbanized lives. Javad, too, was deeply troubled by the remaking of Tehran. He worked as a senior engineer on many of the capital's leading development projects, and his life's ambition had been to build a modern city with gleaming hospitals and telecommunications towers.

Javad and I first met in 1974, when I was twenty-seven, at the home of family friends. A few weeks later, he walked into my Tehran courtroom wearing a white suit and pretended to need my opinion on an obscure legal question. He was an electrical engineer whose work didn't involve fine points of civil law, but he was keen for us to get to know each other.

I appreciated his initiative. Back in those days, many parents insisted on picking out their children's partners, but my parents were open-minded and were happy for me to make my own decisions. As Javad and I spent evenings together in the restaurants of Tehran in those early days of courtship, it became clear that he was at ease with my independence and appreciated my blunt, willful character. This mattered deeply to me, because many Iranian men were not so receptive to a woman with a demanding career. In the 1970s, many Iranian women from upper-middle-class, educated families pursued careers, but traditional attitudes about women's duty to home life had scarcely budged. Javad, though, seemed to find it the most natural thing in the world that I was a judge. He appreciated my independence, and I was attracted to his self-confidence. We were married on a spring day, with the head prosecutor of the judiciary as one of our witnesses. I carried a bouquet of white roses.

Since then, despite all the tumult we'd experienced,

our marriage had been solid. When I stopped practicing law, Javad was supportive, just as he was in the early 1990s, when I began to take on human rights cases. We had our two daughters to raise and our cottage, with its small orchard, as a refuge; we had our parents and siblings. And though our interests differed—Javad was athletic and enjoyed playing classical Persian instruments, while I worked long hours and went hiking with poet friends—even once our daughters were grown, our marriage had a solidarity that we both treasured, an accumulated store of shared understandings and private jokes and mutual concerns.

The authorities had monitored me closely since the 1990s, when my legal defense of women and children started getting national attention. Once when we were having trouble with our office phone lines, an electrician took the cover off the phone socket in the wall and found two listening devices, bugs as small as watch batteries, attached to the wires. He removed them with pliers and held them up in the air, a look of disbelief on his face.

"Do you want me to go through all the sockets in the office, *khanoum*?" he asked.

"No, it's fine. Let them listen."

I didn't mind them eavesdropping on my work conversations. I had nothing to hide. Even before seeing the bugs for myself, I had long known that my phones were tapped. During the three weeks I spent in prison in 2000, my interrogators openly referred to private matters—relationships with friends and minute details of discord among colleagues—they could have gleaned only through spying. After the Nobel, though, the surveillance intensified. The state said it feared for my security and assigned me two full-time bodyguards; they were ostensibly there to protect me, but I knew their real purpose was to monitor my work, to report back on every person I met and spoke with. If Javad and I went out to dinner, they came too, sitting at a nearby table.

The scrutiny compelled us to stay at home more. We made salads together in the evenings and sat around our Formica kitchen table, talking about Javad's latest engineering project—Milad Hospital, to be the largest in the capital—and my latest cases. Now when I came home in the evenings, I would first take off my head scarf, then pull the battery out of my mobile phone. Mobile phones, even when switched off, could be used as listening devices. Like many Iranian families, we shared a building with relatives, and when I visited my mother in her apartment one floor beneath ours, as I did most evenings after dinner, I wondered if they had also bugged her rooms, monitoring the movements and opinions of a seventy-year-old woman.

It left me especially uneasy to know that someone was always listening in on my conversations with my children. My older daughter, Negar, was studying for a master's degree at McGill University in Canada, and I spoke to her on the phone every day. One night, not long after I had received the Nobel, the phone rang at around three o'clock in the morning. I grasped for it on my nightstand, knocking over the alarm clock and waking Javad. My heart thudded as I hit the button to answer, wondering what had happened. I always worried about them in the back of my mind, my husband and my daughters, because I was aware that the regime would never hesitate to use them against me. I had known this since that day in 1999 when I was going through the government files for a case I was preparing on behalf of the family of two murdered dissidents and I saw my name on the list of targets for state assassination. It was perhaps the single most terrifying moment of my life, but I thanked God many times afterward for the chance to have seen that list. It showed me the ruthlessness I was up against and primed me for how strong and guarded I would, in turn, need to be.

"What's wrong?" I asked, without saying hello.

"Nothing! I mean, I'm sorry for calling so late. But Behnood asked me to marry him tonight. I wanted you to be the first to know."

I sank back against my pillow and breathed deeply, waving my free hand to indicate to Javad that it was nothing. Behnood was a young Iranian I had met once in Canada while visiting Negar. I knew they liked each other, but he had moved to the United States to pursue a PhD at Georgia Tech.

"But Behnood is in Georgia," I said.

As with all determined young people in love, Negar had already charted the path ahead. She had contacted the university and learned that there was a good chance that she could receive funding to do graduate work there as well. I tried to sound encouraging and pleased for her, but her plan worried me. What if she didn't get admitted? What if she didn't receive scholarship funding? Would she have to walk away from love or quit her studies and move to Georgia, in the hopes of eventually getting into a nearby university? After we said goodbye, I switched the light off and sank back under the covers, leaving the resolution of the issue to God. Fortunately, not long after, news came that Negar had been admitted to Georgia Tech, and she would soon head to Georgia, where she and Behnood would start their life together.

There was only one small complication. They needed to get married fast, as Negar would be entering the United States on a student visa, and at the time, the U.S. government offered Iranian students only single-entry visas. This meant that the thousands of young Iranians who moved to the United States each year to attend university or do graduate study were effectively marooned there, unable to visit their families in Iran for however long it took them to finish their education. All the years of enmity between Iran and the United States hadn't cooled the eagerness of young Iranians to study in America, but it imposed terrible hardships on those who did. As always with politics, it was ordinary people who suffered most when their governments quarreled. For Negar and Behnood, getting married in the United States was not an option either, as there was no prospect of Behnood's parents and relatives receiving American visas to travel for the wedding.

Early that summer, Negar flew back to Tehran. We held her wedding in a large orchard on the outskirts of Tehran, for this was the only place we could have a mixed wedding party. Most of the city's middle-class couples either got married at home or rented out one of these private wedding orchards, which were specially set up with gazebos and catering facilities for receptions. By law, the city's hotels and restaurants were not permitted to allow men and women to mix together, even for a wedding party, and the authorities often raided receptions and parties in private homes in Tehran, fining and arresting guests or demanding bribes.

The night of the wedding, I lingered at the edge of the festivities for a moment to watch my daughter. Javad soon joined me, a gentle smile on his face. We stood there together in the warm night, the buzzing of the crickets audible during a pause in the music of the dance floor, and a thought passed unsaid between us: *It all turned out all right.*

I gave my gratitude to God, and prayed that he would continue to protect us from those who wished us harm.

CHAPTER 3

The Man Who Wanted
to Buy a Centrifuge

♦

In most Iranian cities there is at least one artificial limb shop, for the country has the second highest number of land mines in the world studded into its soil. An estimated sixteen million mines are left over from the war with Iraq, waiting to explode beneath an unsuspecting farmer or child. The government has not done nearly enough to address the land mine problem, and to cover up this neglect it also censors news coverage of land mine deaths and mutilations. As a result, most Iranians who live outside the worst-afflicted regions have little idea that their country harbors such dangers.

This is why I established the Mine Clearing Collaboration Association, the first such NGO in Iran. My primary aim was to make land mines a daily topic; in my experience, when a fringe problem becomes a national problem that people are aware of and discuss in

daily conversations, solutions emerge, and pressure
also mounts on the government to take some action.
The state could pursue mine removal more seriously,
and it could also join the Ottawa Convention, which
demands that states halt the production and deploy-
ment of land mines. Another aim of the organization
was to provide financial help to the injured and
wounded, as many of the hardest-hit areas are also
quite poor, and the cost of the prosthetics themselves,
along with the loss of the ability to work, can be devastating for families. Gradually the Iranian public became more exposed to the issue. The problem in the
ground had become a problem on people's minds, and
I was hopeful that the government would start dealing
more proactively with mine removal.

On a cloudy afternoon in February 2004, a middle-
aged man came to my personal law office, on the ground
floor of my apartment building, and identified himself
as a government official. He was accompanied by a man
he introduced as an American colleague, a professor
from Stanford University. I offered both of them a cup
of tea and some raisin cookies, and the official explained to me in detail how the government was deeply
committed to tackling the land mine crisis; however,
he noted, serious obstacles had emerged around the
procurement of advanced mine-removal equipment.
The most technologically effective demining tools, he
said, qualified as "dual-use" goods, meaning that Iran
could also use them for military purposes, and therefore international sanctions made it impossible for the

state to import such devices. He insisted that this challenge was at the core of the government's difficulties in removing mines.

I listened patiently, leaning into the beige floral upholstery of the armchair, wondering where the conversation would lead. The man stated that he had long-standing expertise in demining and that he had personally designed a device that would work effectively to detect mines on the desert terrain of Iran's western provinces.

"The trouble is, I need to purchase one of the key components abroad, but none of the manufacturers are prepared to sell to me," he said. "They don't trust the government with such a part."

The American, the official explained, was going to assist in the production of the mine-detection equipment. But he did not speak Persian, and he sat impassively listening to our conversation.

"If you, Khanoum Ebadi, would be able to place the order for this component, I would certainly cover all the costs," the official said.

"What exactly is the problem with this component?" I asked.

"Well, it can be used for making centrifuges."

At that time, Iran's nuclear program and all its associated technical complications were not matters of daily debate in the media, so the term "centrifuge" didn't immediately connote anything for me.

"Centrifuges can have a military use, and these American sanctions end up making it impossible for us to procure things we need. If we had this part, Iran would be able to manufacture its own very effective mine-detection machines. Imagine how quickly we could then remove mines."

The American shifted his long legs. He said nothing to signal that he understood what was being said about his country's role in our country's demining problems.

"Could you write the name of this component down for me," I asked, handing the official a piece of paper. I promised that I would talk to some friends who might be able to help, and I said I would do whatever I could in the service of my country.

The two men thanked me and headed out to a waiting taxi. I sat alone in my office holding the scrap of paper, listening to the faint sound of the radio coming from the apartment above. There was an uneasiness in the pit of my stomach. I had started the land mine NGO in order to do something so that children would stop getting blown up while playing in the fields. My feelings about this cause were fierce, because these were such senseless deaths and injuries, entirely preventable if the government would only enact better policies. Now it seemed like I was in a position to take a tangible action. But there was something peculiar about the two men, the silent, tall American from Stanford and the official who so desperately needed this part.

A week later, when I was in Paris attending a seminar, I spoke to my old friend Dr. Karim Lahidji, who would later become the chairman of the International Federation for Human Rights, about the men and their request. He advised me not to get involved in such dealings and, instead, to focus on helping those injured by land mines. Because I had no technical expertise in such matters, it seemed like sensible advice. Besides, I had no idea where I would even begin the search to buy—in bulk, at that—some obscure part that could fit into a centrifuge.

When I returned to Tehran, the official rang to ask for another meeting. I explained that it was simply too complicated for me to find a seller of the part he needed. He never contacted me again. Why an American had been involved, and who he was, I will never know. Perhaps I should have been savvier at the time; but it was only a few years later, when the nuclear dispute truly turned into international news and it became commonplace to read about the West's concern with Iran's nuclear centrifuges, that it occurred to me that the strange men might have been intelligence agents. They had sought to exploit my international stature to carry out a shady transaction, buying banned parts from the West that they were unable to procure themselves. Had they intended to entrap me, or did they simply hope to use me to acquire a part that was proving hard to secure? Although I like to think that the surveillance and harassment I've endured over the years has made me watchful, always on the lookout for odd coincidences and interactions that reveal the hand of Iranian intelligence trying to get close to me, the land mine venture took me by surprise. It showed me that no matter how alert I kept myself, the Islamic Republic would scheme and machinate in ways that I could never anticipate. And it was only going to get worse.

Although my land mine initiative cast me in the government's path, it also yielded an extraordinary opportunity. When Nobel Peace laureate Jody Williams, who won the prize in 1997 for her work on land mines, noticed that I was also working on this cause, she invited me to the 2004 conference of the International Campaign to Ban Landmines, held in Nairobi. I gave a speech about land mines and briefed the conference participants about the situation in Iran. Another speaker was Wangari Maathai, a Kenyan who won the Nobel Peace Prize in 2004, the year after me, for her activities in the field of environment protection, including her campaign against the destruction of trees in Africa.

So, purely by coincidence, we three women Nobel Peace laureates found ourselves in the same place at the same time. I suggested to Jody and Wangari that we join together and start an institute that would harness our activities and work as women peace laureates to improve women's conditions across the world. They were both enthusiastic, and the three of us appeared before journalists holding each other's hands high up in the air. Apart from Aung San Suu Kyi, who at the time was under house arrest, all the other living women laureates were on board with the proposal, and we formally launched the Nobel Women's Initiative in 2006. It was a community of women I felt honored to be a part of and that would prove, in the future, an indispensible help to my work in Iran.

One afternoon in the spring of 2005, I drove to Evin Prison to visit some of my clients. Evin sits close to the base of the Alborz Mountains, and it was one of those clear days when the mountains towered over the city, a hulk of pristine white snow above the brown, slushy streets. As the car turned down the street toward the prison, past low-slung, cement apartment buildings and the white honeycombed block that was the old Hilton Hotel, I pushed my own faded memories of Evin out of my mind. The prison is where I spent three weeks in detention in 2000, after a court charged me with spreading evidence of the state's complicity in an attack on students the previous year. That day I remembered how after my release, my childhood stutter, overcome only in my teenage years with great effort and the help of a psychologist, had returned. I saw a therapist for some weeks and did some exercises, and I managed to overcome it again, but the jolt of having that old affliction resurface never left me.

Walking toward the prison doors, I tried to focus on the clients I was going to visit. Most of them no longer had outstanding legal cases, but like most other human rights lawyers, I still stopped in once or twice a month to keep their spirits up, to see how they were doing and

to occasionally pass them messages from friends or relatives. My persistence in meeting these prisoners
seemed to irritate the state. Just two weeks prior, I had
received a summons to appear before a revolutionary
court. The letter itself did not specify what, if any,
charges the court was considering against me. This
contravened the country's penal code, and I chose to
defy the order. Not much happened after that; a judiciary spokesman told reporters that the revolutionary
court had sent the summons in error, and that a public
court would deal with the matter. I never heard about
it again.

That day as I sat in Evin's waiting room, I saw a
small, wiry man with fierce eyes lurking about the corridor. It was Akbar Ganji, a prominent reformist journalist who had been imprisoned for his investigative
articles that uncovered state complicity in a string of
assassinations. Like many reformists, he had come
from within the very belly of the system, a former Revolutionary Guardsman who had somehow been transformed into the Islamic Republic's Bob Woodward,
responsible for the investigative journalism that shook
the state's very foundations. In 2000 the authorities
arrested him for allegedly violating press laws and un-
dermining national security and sentenced him to ten
years in prison. Now, forgotten inside Evin, he seemed
to be expecting no one. I had noticed him once or twice
before in the waiting room, similarly unoccupied.

"You've been sitting in prison for four and a half

years—how come there's never anyone here to talk to you? Where's your lawyer?" I asked.

"My lawyer didn't even say hello to me last time I saw them."

"Do you want us to take over your case? We could always try for another appeal."

His eyes lit up, and he moved forward.

I opened my briefcase and wrote out a power-of-attorney document on the spot. Ganji signed it, and we took on his case.

I saw him three or four times after becoming his lawyer. One afternoon, when I visited to bring him a book, he told me he was planning to go on hunger strike. After he announced that, the prison authorities wouldn't let me see him anymore.

Ganji's strike started to draw international attention, and Saeed Mortazavi, Tehran's prosecutor general at the time, was furious. Perhaps more than any other official in living memory, Mortazavi is associated in the minds of the public with abuse and the punishment of dissidents and critics. He is suspected by some to have been involved in the 2003 prison assault on Iranian-Canadian photojournalist Zahra Kazemi, who later died of her injuries, although he was never prosecuted. Most journalists and politicians who passed through his courts in those years have stories of the cruel and often idiotic things he said to them in court. I think it would be fair to say that he did not particularly appreciate me as a lawyer.

A couple of days into the hunger strike, Mortazavi publicly told reporters that hunger strikes were illegal under Iranian law and that as a result, the authorities were denying Ganji visitations and phone calls as punishment. This was untrue. The next time a journalist called me to ask about the case, I raised the issue of Bobby Sands Street. In 1981, the new Islamic authorities had renamed Churchill Boulevard, which ran along the British embassy, Bobby Sands Street, in honor of the IRA hunger striker, whom the revolutionaries celebrated as a "freedom fighter."

"Why have the authorities named one of the most important streets of Tehran after Bobby Sands?" I asked. "How come outside the country a hunger strike is heroic and brave, but it is forbidden inside Iran?"

At this, Judge Mortazavi grew livid. He filed a complaint against me, accusing me of spreading lies, and ordered a restriction on my movements, forbidding me to leave Tehran.

And then he shifted his line, arguing that Ganji was not on a hunger strike at all. The talk of a hunger strike was just my invention, he claimed, and Ganji was sitting in prison fit and content.

I challenged this: "Then prove it. Let me visit him and confirm."

The authorities didn't let me visit Ganji. But a sympathetic prison official took a photo of his emaciated frame lying in a prison hospital bed, and the image went viral. In the photo Ganji lies with his head on a lilac pillow, his arms spindly like a small boy's, his skin patchy and sallow. I did all I could, as was so often the case when legally I had no recourse; I gave interviews and led a media campaign, trying to conjure international outrage. When Ganji's wife finally saw him, she told me he looked like a dead man who sometimes moved.

What Ganji's emaciated, broken frame symbolized on that hospital bed was more than one man's willingness to give his life for change. To me, it signified a wider desperation that millions of Iranians felt with the system. Eight years of a reformist presidency, the tenure of Mohammad Khatami, had ended in this. At the most fervent moments in that reformist period, when people had believed that the system could change peacefully from within, Ganji had been at the forefront of the effort. There is a photo of him standing on a pedestrian bridge above the Seventh of Tir Square, near the headquarters of the newspaper from which he had launched his investigations. He smiles broadly, with the traffic streaming beneath him, an impish gleam in his eyes. But now, in 2005, Ganji was a shell. The newspaper was closed, I was not even permitted to visit him, and Khatami's term was over. Many people I spoke to wondered why they should even vote in the upcoming presidential election, when it seemed as though nothing would change.

CHAPTER 4

A Midnight Visit

♦

On the eve of the 2005 presidential election, I was calmly cleaning parsley and cilantro in a sink full of water so I could cook one of the favorite dishes of my younger daughter, Nargess, for dinner. My mobile kept ringing. Four times already I had dried my hands to answer it, but this time I let it go. Journalists were calling me from around the world to ask who I would be voting for the next day and who I thought would win.

"I'm not voting for any candidate," I repeated each time. They would then ask if I was boycotting—journalists were ever eager to attach a quick label to one's motivations—and I would try to simply explain my position. Neither of the two main moderate candidates—Mehdi Karroubi, the former speaker of the parliament, and Akbar Hashemi Rafsanjani, the former president—inspired my confidence. I did not believe that their leadership would start Iran down the path I felt it needed to take. Lawfulness, reform, respect for citizens' rights—these were enormous structural problems that required a visionary, not regime loyalists who might be pragmatic but would not fundamentally challenge what was wrong with the system. With one eye on the stove throughout these conversations, I also brought up the problems with the electoral process itself.

At the time, Iran was unique in the region for having competitive elections. Throughout most of the Middle East, dictators either didn't hold elections at all or held farcical events, ignored by their people, in which they won 99.9 percent of the vote. In Iran, there is enough political rivalry, and enough of a constitutional mandate for an electoral process, that elections draw a reasonable turnout, and rarely since the 1979 revolution has the result been wholly or even partially known beforehand. Iran's elections have largely been clean, if only because the process of vetting candidates is itself dirty: high clerical authorities vet candidates and permit only those figures they consider acceptable to make it onto the ballot. As a result, there is real rivalry between some figures, but it is not a truly democratic process by any stretch. I told the journalists calling that night that I did not consider this a fair enough process and could not see myself participating.

When the phone began ringing again, I looked at it with some frustration, but then I noticed that the caller was Nargess. She was on her way home from Bagh-e

Gilas, a café in northern Tehran that she and her friends frequented. Nargess was still living at home; though she had been admitted to McGill University in Canada to study international law, I had persuaded her to first sit for the bar exam in Tehran, then move abroad. In order to become a fully licensed lawyer in Iran, you must first pass the bar, then complete an apprenticeship, so she had a gap year before starting in Canada. In my dreams, she would finish her PhD and return to Iran to work alongside me to defend human rights cases. But I knew that, like her sister, she had other visions for her life.

Some young people are better able to tolerate the duplicity and compromises that living in Iran demands of them. But Nargess had always found the state's social restrictions and the bullying atmosphere difficult. She was an exuberant young woman, talkative and quick to joke and laugh. She hated when I told her not to laugh so loudly in public—I didn't want her to attract the attention of the morality police, but she still felt indignant at being scolded for such a natural behavior. She had a profound sense of justice and chafed at unfair restrictions. One of her favorite pastimes with her girlfriends was to go to a local coffee shop for milk shakes. The owners, under orders from the municipality, permitted customers to linger for only one hour, before turning them out. Her girlfriends were often happy to simply move on to another café, but Nargess had never made peace with such restrictions. She saw them for what they were: an unfair policy designed to interfere with young people's lives. She was always the one to demand why, the one to push back. She had been like this from the beginning, even as a child. During Ramazan, when the state forbade eating in public, she would always complain at having to hide her head in my handbag to take a bite from a sandwich.

"There's so much traffic," she said, and I could hear cars honking in the background. "I'll be later than I thought." And then the call dropped before I could reply, as it so often did in Tehran. Nargess was not planning to vote, and neither were others in our family. On these kinds of matters we were mostly in agreement.

Finally Nargess arrived, followed shortly after by Javad, and we had one of those family dinners that at the time seemed ordinary: the three of us sitting around the kitchen table, the light glowing softly against the linoleum pattern of the floor, the sheen of the navy cotton cloth beneath our plates. We talked about Negar, who was about to move to Georgia, and Nargess's own plans to study law. We helped ourselves to pickled vegetables from the cobalt-blue ceramic bowl we had bought in Kashan, on a summer trip when the girls were small. These details linger in my mind when I look back now, a reminder of the sheer beauty of the present, which we so rarely appreciate.

It was a testament to how little Mahmoud Ahmadinejad featured in the national political debate that we didn't speak about him that night at dinner. His name didn't come up, as no one thought he stood a chance. It

was only later that people started paying attention to
what Ahmadinejad had been up to that week.

We went to bed that night having heard that Mehdi
Karroubi was ahead, and woke up to learn that because
no one had received 50 percent of the vote, the election would be determined in a second round. The two
finalists were Rafsanjani and, unbelievably, Mahmoud
Ahmadinejad. We stood in our pajamas absorbing this
astonishing news. I boiled water and absently stirred
Nescafé into a cup of hot milk. Until that moment,
Ahmadinejad's campaign, which had attracted modest
attention only in the final few days, had seemed mostly
a gimmick. He had started appearing in small towns
across Iran wearing a faded windbreaker and complaining that the rich political elite were exploiting the
downtrodden poor. "I'll bring the country's oil wealth
to the people's dinner tables," he had promised, por-
traying himself, despite the enormous influence he
enjoyed as mayor of Tehran, as one of the people, a
modest figure in an old jacket.

"Maybe people in small towns and villages voted for
him?" I suggested to Javad as we sat down to breakfast.
Urban intellectuals and reformists weren't exactly well
attuned to rural and small-town Iran. But since the
country was 70 percent urbanized, it was not as though
the rural areas could have dominated a national election.

Although the necessity for a runoff was worrisome,
no one imagined that the second round would produce
anything but a Rafsanjani victory. When Ahmadinejad

won a few days later, we were shocked. Rafsanjani declared that the election had been tampered with, and
he said that because he knew that no one—by this he
meant the supreme leader—would pay attention to his
grievances, he would complain only to God.

Some months later, the reformist faction in the parliament published findings that showed how Ahmadinejad had spent public money from the Tehran
municipality on his election campaign. It wasn't clear
yet what implications Ahmadinejad's win would have
for Iran, but he was religiously conservative and politically hard-line, the kind of Iranian politician who was
suspicious of the West to the point of paranoia. He was
also obsessed with making daily life more religious,
against the wishes of the majority of Iranians. It seemed
most likely that for us, the lawyers at the Defenders of
Human Rights Center, and our work, his presidency
would not augur well.

Not long after the election, my older daughter, Negar,
arrived for her last visit before starting her studies in
Georgia. Her arrival always involved an intense sched-
ule of socializing, as all the relatives wanted to see her
and she also wanted to see her friends from high school;
the result was typically two weeks packed with family
lunches and dinner parties. One night the girls and I
had dinner at a cousin's house and took a taxi home
after midnight. As we got out, two young men stepped
out of the shadows of a nearby building.

"Mrs. Ebadi?" one of them said. Their hair was slicked back with gel, and one wore a baggy plaid blazer, under which something seemed to be bulging.

"Yes, and yourself?" I replied curtly. I was aware of my two daughters behind me, their party dresses covered only by light overcoats.

"We've come to see you about a legal matter," said the one in the blazer, moving too close. "Can we impose on your time?"

"Legal matters are handled during the day, by appointment. You can call my office tomorrow."

"But we've come a long way," the other young man called out, taking a few steps forward.

At that precise moment, the doors of a nearby restaurant flung open and people began pouring out into the street. They were dressed up and clearly coming from a wedding reception, and within minutes there were nearly a hundred people outside, talking and looking for taxis and cars. The two men who had approached us looked startled, and edged aside.

"Good night to you," I said, without even turning back. The three of us turned together and began walking away.

Once we were inside the house, the girls hung up their coats and head scarves and were soon back to laughing and chatting and dissecting the party, as though nothing had happened. I watched them unbuckle their sandal straps, their nails painted in shades that matched their dresses. But my spirits had dived. I didn't believe for a moment that those two men had wanted to discuss a case with me. I had spent years fielding visits from distressed family members of people who needed legal help; they were quick to launch into their stories and unfailingly polite. These men had seemed sanguine and pushy. And they had been waiting at the top of my street after midnight on a weekend when both of my daughters happened to be with me. They had come, I was convinced, to try to hurt me in some way. I moved silently into my bedroom, more angry than scared. I remembered what one of the interrogators had said to me when I was imprisoned in Evin. It had only been three weeks in solitary confinement, but the girls had been younger then, and I had been desperate to get out.

"Don't you miss your daughters?" he had asked, looking at me with contempt, as though I had done something terrible to land myself in a prison, not only a criminal but a neglectful mother.

I didn't fall asleep that night until very late, and twice I tiptoed down the hall to peer into the room where the girls slept.

Iran's Interior Ministry is located in a looming brown 1970s-style building on Fatemi Street, named for Hossein Fatemi, the politician who in the early 1950s helped Prime Minister Mohammad Mossadegh nationalize Iranian oil and gas. This bold initiative made Mossadegh a national hero, and the 1953 CIA-orchestrated coup that toppled his government was a devastating moment for my generation of Iranians. We lost our much-beloved, democratically elected leader, we lost our sense of inviolability and independence, and we lost our nationalist aspirations. In their place, we gained the conviction that the United States wished Iran harm. After the coup, the shah's men arrested Fatemi and executed him by firing squad. In the wake of the 1979 revolution, most of the city's streets had been renamed after Shia saints, Islamic revolutionaries, or, later, war martyrs, but Fatemi had remained Fatemi. My family, like many in Iran, had been closely affected by the coup and its legacy. My father had been an ardent supporter of Mossadegh's, and after 1953 he lost his senior position in the Ministry of Agriculture, returning only years later to a succession of low-level jobs. I had often thought of him when I lost my judgeship, and of how Iran's history might have unfolded differently had Mossadegh not been tripped by the United States just as he sought to move the country down the path of true independence.

I walked up the steps to the ministry, watching the warm breeze of the early Tehran summer make the Islamic Republic flag flutter. I was there to visit Abdolvahed Moussavi Lari, the outgoing interior minister, to discuss why the Defenders of Human Rights Center had not yet received its official permit. We had founded the center in 2001, and legally the constitution did not oblige us to request a state license for our activities. But as with much of everything that went on in Iran, the authorities applied and invoked the law selectively, molding it to fit their political aims and, often, to quiet their opponents. I was not an opponent of the state—I was a human rights defender, and I based my criticisms of the state on legal grounds. But authoritarian governments are not fond of shades of gray; they cannot tolerate any criticism at all, and so I knew that at some stage, the authorities might quibble with the center's status.

We had applied for a formal permit soon after our founding and had begun our activities while we waited. Four years had passed, and still no permit; I knew that an order had been given at the Interior Ministry to grant one, but the actual certificate had never materialized. When I had chased this two years prior, an official had told me, "You're carrying on with your work, no one is bothering you. Why do you need a piece of paper?" Perhaps I was being stubborn, but years of dealing with the Islamic Republic had taught me that legal vagueness meant legal vulnerability. I wanted that piece of paper. I pressed, and the official promised to give us our license the following week. But that week became two years, and now, in June 2005, we still had no certificate. With Ahmadinejad set to take office, this last week of Khatami's presidency seemed like a smart time to make a final push.

As I announced myself to Lari's staff, I noticed a striking absence of women. Everywhere there were young and old men answering phones, seated behind computers, but not a single woman among them. In Tehran, this was rare enough to be conspicuous. Though women rarely ascended to senior or manage-

rial positions in ministries, they were usually well represented among the lower-level staff. Apart from this,
Lari's office was like that of any other minister: spacious but spare, with a small sitting area in one corner
of the room.

I sat down opposite the minister, who was a cleric
and wore a black turban, the designation for those who
are descendants of the prophet Muhammad. There was
a calendar on his desk with a panoramic photo of the
turquoise mosque in Isfahan, and a heavy glass paper-
weight.

"Why don't you give us our license?" I asked bluntly.
"If you happen to get sent to prison over some political
disagreement in the future, who's going to defend you?
You should keep the center working for such a rainy
day!"

He smiled at this but shook his head confidently.
"Such a day will never come," he said. But he told me
that we could have our license. I sat there listening to
him direct his assistant to follow up on this; then he
told me, "You'll be contacted very soon."

I had heard those words too many times to imagine
that they meant anything. And, of course, after I left
his office, nothing happened. Perhaps the reformists
were not overly fond of us; we had recorded their of-
fenses and legal breaches in many of our reports. But
despite our presence as a sort of permanent spike in
their side, they tolerated us. They tolerated me and my
colleagues, and in their time, our work was still a part
of Iran.

I went home straight after the meeting, as I was expecting a visitor that evening. Ahmed Chalabi, the
Iraqi politician who had helped persuade the United
States to topple Saddam Hussein, had asked to meet
with me. Chalabi was close to the Iranian government
as well, and I found it strange that there had been no
mention of his arrival in the Iranian media. When the
hour of our appointment came and went, my phone
rang. It was Chalabi; speaking in reasonably good Persian, he apologized for not being able to come in person. He had wanted to meet with me, he explained, to
ask whether I would consider serving as a judge in Saddam Hussein's trial. The U.S. military had captured
Saddam at the end of 2003, and he had remained in
detention since then, awaiting trial for the various
atrocities he committed during his long years running
Iraq, from using chemical weapons against Iraqi Kurds
to crushing the Shia villages in Iraq's south.

"You can't try him in Iraq," I said. "He needs to
be tried in an international criminal court, a proper
tribunal."

"But a tribunal won't hand down a death sentence,"
he said.

"Well, if you're determined to execute him in advance of a trial, I can't be a part of that."

Our conversation ended there. It would have been
powerful and politically deeply symbolic to have had an
Iranian woman judge, a Shia, presiding over the fate of
Saddam Hussein. But I could not participate in a kan-
garoo court, when it was precisely that sort of abroga-

tion of justice I had spent my life in Iran challenging. I saw no mention in the Iranian papers in the following days that Chalabi had visited Tehran, and I thought it remarkable that the United States had relied so heavily on a man who had such intimate ties with the Iranian government. A man who passed through Tehran without a trace, and spoke Persian well enough to negotiate on his own.

CHAPTER 5

In the Shadow of
Ahmadinejad

♦

In September 2005, not many weeks into his presidency, Ahmadinejad walked up to the podium at the
United Nations General Assembly and declared that
Iran had the right to nuclear power and would defy
America's "nuclear apartheid." He ended his address
with a prayer, predicting that the last imam of Shia
Islam would soon emerge. Watching this from my living
room in Tehran, I felt a sense of dread. His disingenu-
ous smirk, his look of almost pleased indifference as
world leaders regarded him with distaste and dismay—
I saw that this man relished confrontation, and that his
political ideology registered this defiance as a great success. I recall that moment with particular clarity even
now, because that was when the anxiety I would constantly hold in my body first set in, the growing aware-

ness that things looked poised to go badly, perhaps even disastrously wrong.

The reformists had tolerated my work as a human rights defender, and during their tenure Iran had been on relatively stable terms with the world. Not good terms, but stable ones. The West had serious griev- ances with Iran's behavior in the region and was trou- bled by the country's nuclear program. But Iran, until Ahmadinejad, had not actively been looking for a fight. Though he had promised to improve the country's economy and bring better living conditions to the working poor, both in the cities and in rural areas, the new president now seemed mostly interested in throw- ing Iran onto a collision course with the West.

As Iran stumbled into this uncertain new era, one consolation was that my daughter Nargess was still liv- ing at home. My elderly mother had died in late 2004, as well as my beloved older sister, Mina, who had been ill with cancer. Having Nargess around after these losses was a great salve. She would often spread her law books out on the table in the evenings, and we would work together side by side, one of us occasionally rising to pour more tea or bring out a bowl of dried mulberries. On some evenings, Javad practiced his *tar,* a traditional Iranian string instrument, in the other corner of the living room; on other nights he would return from a singing class and find us with our heads bent over our work. "How diligent mother and daughter both are," he would often say fondly, dropping a kiss on Nargess's head. Our marriage was more companionable now that the girls were young adults.

Nargess was now interning at the Iranian Bar Association. When she had studied law at Shahid Beheshti University, a top law school, I had looked over her assignments and coursework with curiosity, to see how law was being taught under the Islamic Republic. When I had been a law student, in the 1960s, we had carefully studied key principles of Islamic sharia, despite the fact that the shah had instituted a secular criminal and civil code. After the revolution, one would have expected the universities to expand and enhance their teaching of sharia, since the new regime had replaced the shah's secular legal system with Islamic law. But Nargess was learning less than half of what I had learned about sharia principles in my own student days. Why was this the case? Essentially because the crafters of the Islamic Republic's education system did not want to teach students the subtleties of sharia law, philosophy, and tradition. Well-trained and erudite students would be equipped to argue for fresher and more modern angles and approaches to Islamic laws. But the Islamic Republic wanted dim Muslims who were not literate in Islamic legal debates, for Muslims who knew their religion could be potential enemies of the regime. This is why a fundamentalist cleric once said in his address to the country's parliament, "We need jurists who are committed to the Islamic Republic and should not be educating and delivering to society people like Shirin Ebadi."

To the likely dismay of that cleric, the volume of my work was growing all the time. I was constantly giving interviews, meeting new clients, and generally functioning more than ever as a repository for those seeking justice. Most often people would come to me after they had lost hope of securing a fair outcome through the courts, and I found myself repeating the same phrases to nearly everyone who passed through my door: "The courts in our country are no longer independent, so you shouldn't be too hopeful. I can't perform miracles, but I will make use of all the channels and loudspeakers at my disposal to convey your voice to the rest of the world."

In the evenings, Nargess and I would often interrupt our work to watch the news, both the state broadcaster's newscast and the BBC Persian service, to learn what was transpiring around the world. The state news often carried images of Ahmadinejad's trips around the country. Inevitably the camera would follow him as he shook the hands of grizzled old farmers in some drought-stricken part of Iran, the cracked, yellow dirt forming a landscape of utter devastation that Ahmadinejad, now portrayed as a national hero, was promising to rescue. During his visits, Ahmadinejad would give speeches to a rural crowd overcome with admiration, he would wave their letters of complaint before the camera, promising state accountability, and he would then walk through the crowd passing around envelopes of cash, each holding 100,000 *tomans* (the equivalent, then, of about $50).

This infusion of cash into the economy was dangerously inflationary. The country's economists were appalled. They published letters in national newspapers warning of impending economic crisis; even the head of the Central Bank of Iran warned that Ahmadinejad's policies would cause rampant inflation. But their complaints resonated nowhere, and ordinary, impoverished Iranians, understandably, viewed Ahmadinejad, with his impassioned rural speeches and fat envelopes of cash, as some sort of savior. The envelopes, much like a drug habit, offered a balm to hardship in the short term, but they created a far greater problem for the country's treasury down the line.

During the first two years of his initial four-year term as president, Ahmadinejad enjoyed great freedom—he had the unconditional support of the supreme leader, whom the Iranian constitution vests with absolute power, and the backing of the country's hard-line establishment. When the clerics had taken over Iran in 1979 and devised a legal system that vested them with absolute power, the running of the economy had ranked low among their priorities. The Ayatollah Khomeini famously said, "This revolution was not about the price of watermelons," and his successor, Ayatollah Khamenei, seemed similarly unfazed by Ahmadinejad's economic shenanigans.

Apart from seducing the rural and urban poor with cash handouts, Ahmadinejad was also adept at nurturing Iranians' inherent sense of nationalism. One evening, as we were all gathered in the living room watching the news, the state television station broadcast Ahmadinejad giving a speech about the country's promising young scientists. He claimed, "There's a girl who went to her high school principal and told her, '*Khanoum,* I've discovered nuclear energy at home, can you do something with this?'" Ahmadinejad then went on to describe how he had dispatched scientists from the Atomic Energy Organization of Iran to check out the purported discovery. "They went to her house, and they saw that in the kitchen, with parts she'd bought at the bazaar, and with some help from her big brother, she had actually produced nuclear energy!"

I watched, dumbfounded, and turned to look at Javad and Nargess, who both appeared stunned as well. It was one of the moments, of which there were too many in Iran, when we didn't know whether to laugh or cry. It was truly hilarious, what the president was claiming: that a high school girl had cooked up nuclear fission in her kitchen. But it was also profoundly disturbing, the extent to which the president would bend the truth, contort reality, in order to persuade Iranians that their country had the right to nuclear power. In a later news broadcast it emerged that Ahmadinejad had sent bodyguards to secure the safety of this budding genius and her kitchen laboratory, though we never learned her name or the precise nature of her astonishing discovery.

It was just after lunch on an ordinary Wednesday when I glanced at the clock and realized it was nearly time for

Mr. Mahdavi, a state intelligence agent, to drop by for his appointment. He came to my office occasionally to discuss various "concerns," always telephoning in advance to set a time, and was studiously polite. I knew that Mahdavi was not his real name—all the state's intelligence agents concealed their real identities—and though his manner was civil, the simple fact that I was dealing with someone with a fake name unsettled me. The previous week I had received a threatening letter in the mail, and I had been considering whether to mention it to Mahdavi. Javad was especially worried, and I felt I had to do something. The letter had read: "If you continue your work, both you and your daughter Nargess will be taken care of."

I hadn't mentioned the letter to Nargess; she already took all the precautions I thought necessary for her safety, and I didn't want her to feel intimidated or, even worse, resentful at such a young age. She would have plenty of time to grow politically bitter later.

Mahdavi might not know anything about the letter, I figured, and perhaps it was better that way. The Iranian state ran various intelligence branches, some much more hard-line than others, and they often competed with each other. If another branch had decided to get tough with me, better for Mahdavi's branch not to feel compelled to match it.

I slipped the papers I had been reviewing into a folder and pulled on a head scarf, waiting for the buzzer. When it rang, it was only a few minutes after the hour, but Mahdavi apologized for his slight tardiness. He was a tidy man of medium build with a clipped beard and a lawyerly demeanor, always jotting down notes on a yellow pad and pressing me for more details.

After a few pleasantries, he raised the latest "concern" he had with my work. In early 2005, I had agreed to represent Roozbeh Mirebrahimi, a journalist and blogger the authorities had arrested in 2004, leveling the various charges they usually brought against reporters who worked for the country's beleaguered but still functioning independent press. In agreeing to represent him, I had repeated publicly that Iran's judicial and penal system was deeply flawed. Mahdavi and his superiors in the Ministry of Intelligence did not appreciate such remarks.

"Khanoum Ebadi, you know what the problem is," he said, crossing his legs and looking at me intently. "America is our enemy, and it takes advantage of such criticisms."

"But what I've said is perfectly true."

"So you should come and tell these things directly to us. Don't go and tell the media. When you do that, the enemy exploits your words."

It was a conversation we had had before, on several occasions. Each time Mahdavi made the same supplications, and I gave him the same replies.

"If the state stops behaving badly, then I won't have anything to say. Then there will be no cause for anyone to exploit anything. But if what I say is being exploited, the root of the problem is the state's behavior."

He looked at me that day with some disappointment. I shrugged, finding I had nothing to add. I had been a judge and was now a lawyer, and the law concerns itself with intent and the results of intent. If the state intended the best for its citizens, then it needed to demonstrate that in its behavior toward them. It could not arrest journalists, throw them in prison, inflict all manner of psychological torture and abuse on them, and then dispatch an agent to talk to me about America "exploiting" my objections to this.

"I can only ask you again: please don't speak in such a way that will harm the regime," Mahdavi said, rising to leave.

When I had closed the door behind him, I sat down at the table, wondering for how much longer they would phrase these demands as requests.

That winter, as 2005 slipped into 2006, Ahmadinejad's net of persecution widened. On a cold February afternoon in the holy city of Qom, a day that happened to be Ashura, the most precious mourning day in Shia Islam, hundreds of Sufis were gathered at a local *hosseiniyeh*, or prayer hall, dressed all in black and weeping for the martyrdom of Imam Hossein, a grandson of the prophet Muhammad who was killed in the seventh-century battle of Karbala and remains a central figure in Shia Islam. The men slapped their chests rhythmically and chanted the mourning cries for Imam Hossein, their voices intermingling and rising together.

Outside the doors of the *hosseiniyeh*, dozens of bearded

men in disheveled clothing, their shirts untucked and their faces taut with anger, prepared to break into the mourning ceremony. When given the word by the militia commander, they pushed the doors open and attacked the mourners. Rushing forward with loud shouts, they shoved and kicked every man they met. The Sufis reeled, many of them falling back, startled out of their trancelike grief. Shots rang out. It was unclear from where, but there were shouts of "He's been shot!," and then it was mayhem, as the attackers and the mourners scattered in every direction.

Not long after all the Sufis had fled, several more men arrived and began planting empty whiskey bottles and women's underwear around the deserted *hosseini-yeh*. There was blood on the floor in places, from those who had been wounded, but they carefully ignored this and concentrated on leaving their incriminating evidence.

Then the bulldozer came. It rumbled down the street and began bashing its cement claw at the front walls. It tore a chunk off the main doorway and then attacked the sides, leaving dusty and jagged holes in its wake. The residents of Qom and hundreds of Sufis poured into the streets to watch smoke billow from the ruins of the *hosseiniyeh*. Within hours, it was ash and rubble. That night, the state television news service announced that despite the sacredness of the holy day of Ashura, the Sufis had converged at their prayer hall to drink alcohol and have illicit sex. This was why, the newscaster said, their *hosseiniyeh* had been demolished.

Just over a year into Ahmadinejad's tenure, his administration and cronies were giving free rein to the religious extremists that filled the ranks of the state's voluntary militias. Though the members of these militias did not draw formal state salaries, they received endless financial perks, from low-interest loans to mortgages to use of government cars. They did not wear uniforms, but they were supported by the state security forces, and they often acted independently of the police. Often the militias mobilized as a vigilante force, breaking up lectures and events they deemed critical of the state, as well as setting up their own morality checkpoints, harassing young people who had Western music or alcohol in their cars, and raiding private parties. While President Khatami was in power, he had sought to rein in the militias, demanding more lawfulness and a respect for people's privacy. But Ahmadinejad reversed this course and instead began egging the militias on, encouraging their most intolerant attitudes and giving them subtle signals that should they wish to punish those who deviated from their strict view of Islam, the state would not get in their way. The Iranian legal system, with the head of its judiciary appointed directly by the supreme leader, worked in tandem with this growing radicalism.

The Sufis, whose mystical practice of Islam emerged in the eighth century, posed no real threat to the state, though their numbers were considerable. The Gonabadi Sufis, who took their name from a region of northeastern Iran where the founder of the sect hailed

from, found meddling in politics abhorrent. They just
wanted to be left alone to practice their Islam, and
across Iran's cities, they went about their lives, as doctors, lawyers, writers, and so on, but chose to worship
in the mode of Sufi ritual. The more hard-line state
clergy and the government did not appreciate the Sufis;
they considered them somehow deviant, just as they
considered anyone who practiced a more tolerant,
more flexible interpretation of Islam deviant. The authorities had banned the Sufis from practicing their
traditional whirling dance, as well as a number of their
most colorful practices, like walking through flames
without getting burned or being pierced without drawing blood.

I knew the leader, or *morshed,* of the Sufis, Mr. Tabandeh, from my days as a judge, before the revolution. It was unthinkable that his followers would have
been drinking and womanizing in a prayer hall, let
alone on the day of Ashura, as all the reports in the
state-controlled newspapers alleged. The independent
newspapers still publishing at the time related the
events more objectively, but even they merely reported
the raid and demolition without investigating what had
really transpired.

A few days later, three people stopped by my office.
They said that a few of the wounded Sufis had lodged a
complaint with the Qom magistrate's court against
some of the assailants, whose identities had been determined, and also the men who had ordered the assault. But when the prosecutor had seen the complaint,

he had refused to register it and order an investigation. Instead, he tore up the document before their eyes and told them that as the guilty parties they had no such legal recourse. When the Sufi leader, Mr. Tabandeh, heard of this, he told them to come to me. "Take the case to Mrs. Ebadi and ask her to represent us. If she is involved, the prosecutor won't dare to tear up the complaint."

I asked my visitors to explain the real cause of the clashes. They said that recently the Sufis had been drawing ever bigger crowds. Iranians who were committed to Islam but alienated from the official mosques, which they associated with state corruption and hypocrisy, were attracted to their order. At the Sufi *hosseiniyeh,* there was no mandatory six-minute prayer for the health of the supreme leader and other senior officials. As a religious alternative, at a time when Iranians were increasingly turning away from mosques and state prayer, the Sufi religion offered a vibrant Islamic alternative.

The people's flocking to the Sufi *hosseiniyeh* had prompted one of Qom's influential clerics, a man who enjoyed the endorsement and affection of the supreme leader, to issue a warning. The cleric, whose own speeches and ceremonies were no longer well attended, had demanded that the *hosseiniyeh* be placed under his authority. The Sufis had refused this, citing the endowment documentations they possessed, which had set out the procedures for the management of the *hosseiniyeh*'s affairs. Ultimately, the simmering envy of a few influential clerics had prompted a group of state-supported vigilantes, along with their clerical backers, to attack the Sufis that day.

I immediately agreed to act as the wounded Sufis' attorney, and I asked two of my colleagues to take on the case with me. One was a lawyer from Qom, Mohammad Seyfzadeh, whose local influence I thought might prove useful. The next day Seyfzadeh visited the office of the prosecutor of the city of Qom, carrying a power-of-attorney letter signed by both of us and the three visitors from Qom. On that occasion, upon seeing my name, the prosecutor did not tear anything up and instead opened a case file. Seyfzadeh, who would later be sentenced to six years in prison for his legal activities, requested that the victims hurt during the attack be examined immediately by a forensic doctor, to document their injuries before they healed. But the court, in a delaying tactic, asked him to return the following day; when he did, he was told that the file had been sent to Tehran to be handled by the Special Court for Clergy. Legally this would not have precluded the victims' examination, but the prosecutor intentionally took his time forwarding the paperwork, so that the wounds would fade with time.

It took two months to refer the case to Tehran, and when I followed up I was told precisely what I had been expecting to hear: that neither I nor any of my colleagues had the right to represent the case, because we were not clerics, and that it would be handled by the Special Court for Clergy. This separate court effectively worked to shield clerics from the law, much as diplomatic immunity protects diplomats from being prosecuted for all manner of wrongdoing. So the final outcome of this disturbing and tragic case had really been determined from the outset. And after that, the state's relations with the Sufis deteriorated sharply. Hundreds of Sufi followers in cities and towns across Iran were arrested, and even this mild, peaceful section of society found itself besieged and imprisoned, made an enemy target by the state.

CHAPTER 6

The Women Who Dared to Rise Up

◆

On June 12, 2006, a cloudless, summery afternoon, a group of women's rights activists began arriving at the Seventh of Tir Square, one of the capital's major public spaces. It is a sprawling, wide square, lined with manteau shops, office buildings, and florists, always busy with traffic, as the motorway that leads north to the city intersects the square to its north. The afternoon was warm, and some of the women wore sandals and light, modest manteaus. Although thick brown smog usually hangs over Seventh of Tir, that day the air was bright, the green patches of grass around the traffic islands looked lush and healthy, and the square bustled with the honking of taxis and the slow rumbling of buses.

Earlier, the activists had crossed the streets of Tehran passing out a pamphlet titled *Why We Don't Consider the Present Laws Just.* The tone of the pamphlet was simple and disarming; in natural language, it used anecdotal examples to illustrate why the country's laws—"which we often don't think about until we fall into a fix"— were so deeply problematic for women. The women had a few banners rolled up in their handbags, but they had not yet removed them, not wishing to attract attention before the crowd properly formed. Around seventy people had arrived and were milling about the central south side of the square, chatting and waiting for others to join. I passed through the square that afternoon, but I didn't stay for the protest itself. That night, the organizers recounted for me what had come to pass.

Just a few minutes before four o'clock, the key organizers, who had arrived early, noticed a small convoy of green-and-white police cars heading down from the north side of the square. As though the moves were coordinated, some motorbikes bearing policemen in riot-gear helmets poured in from a narrow side street to the east of the square. Out of several police vans flooded policewomen in severe, head-to-toe black chadors. They began running through the square, waving batons, the fabric of their chadors billowing around them. The protesters tried to melt into traffic, to scamper toward the sidewalks and into the crowd. But suddenly there were police officers everywhere, shouting for everyone to disperse but not letting anyone get away. The policewomen roughly grabbed women protesters by the arm and dragged them toward the waiting vans. Male police officers attacked the men in the crowd. Great plumes of tear gas shot out, and people screamed, "My eyes, my eyes!" Some women stumbled and doubled over, clutching at their faces.

One particular policewoman, with a heavy build and a brown *maghnaeh,* a cloaklike head covering, was the most violent. She looked almost like an executioner, the activists recounted later, storming about and shouting and digging her nails into the arms of the protesters. Her face, they said, contorted in rage as she strode from assault to assault. When women collapsed from the tear gas, the policewoman grabbed them by their head scarves and dragged them along the pavement toward the police vans.

The authorities put down the protest before it even got started, crushing it with a violence no one had anticipated. They injured a number of the protesters and arrested a number of the key organizers, even Ali Akbar Moussavi Khoeini, a reformist former member of parliament who had come out in solidarity with the women. In the days after the crushed protest, the Tehran public prosecutor declared that the arrested protesters were accused of disturbing public order, fostering tension and unrest, and spreading lies. The police had, of course, known about the protest in advance; the organizers had posted the date and time on their website, for they felt they had nothing to hide. But it was clear that the regime would not tolerate such public gatherings, even if they were peaceful. This directly violated the constitution, which upholds people's right to free assembly and public demonstration, on the condition that no weapons are carried and the principles and tenets of Islam are not undermined. But for the purposes of the organizers, with whom I was in touch, the crackdown and arrests made bruisingly clear that they would need to change tactics.

The activists met shortly afterward to discuss what had happened and to devise a new strategy that the state would tolerate. To be effective meant not crossing certain red lines. A feminist movement that was locked up, imprisoned, and not permitted to organize, they knew, would be of little benefit to anyone. Their experience in the women's movement to that moment pointed to the need for legal reform, but it was the fateful crackdown at Seventh of Tir that actually gave the women their new direction. As I have experienced so often myself, being crushed simply gives you greater exercise in collecting the shards of yourself, putting them back together, and figuring out what to do next.

About a month later, two of the country's most prominent women's rights activists came to my office. The trees outside the building were thick with green leaves, and the sun was shining so brightly that I flicked off the office lights. As Noushin Ahmadi Khorasani and Parvin Ardalan took off their manteaus and head scarves, I poured tea, waiting for the bubbles to settle across the amber liquid. Parvin had a commanding presence, with her mop of curly black hair, huge dark eyes, and winged eyebrows. Noushin was slighter and more unassuming. They were both in their early thirties and had worked for years as journalists and community activists. They seemed more energized than usual that day, and when we sat down around the dark oak table to talk, they explained that they were about to launch an important new campaign.

"It will be called the One Million Signatures campaign," said Noushin. "It will, of course, protest against legal discriminations against women, but it will get us out door-to-door across the country, moving forward the conversation about women's rights."

Both of them looked at me expectantly.

"So, Khanoum Ebadi, do you agree with our idea?" Noushin finally asked. "Can you help us?"

I had been silent because I was so moved. It felt like all the efforts that women like me had made in the early years of the revolution, pushing back against all that discrimination and state bullying, were finally—nearly three decades later—bearing some fruit. Iran's feminist movement was one of the country's most striking features. Despite the state's fierce repressiveness—everything from laws that permitted stoning and polygamy to morality police sweeps that harassed women on the street for not dressing conservatively enough—Iran had a burgeoning, vibrant women's movement. Most important, it had grassroots support among women of all backgrounds. This wasn't a clique of upper-class women who had studied in Europe and were supported by their husbands but a real movement, with centers and seminars and training sessions with titles like "How to Cope with Interrogation." Though it was not something that I particularly wished to take credit for, it did seem that my receipt of the Nobel in 2003 had propelled the women's activists. To have a woman just like them, a woman they knew, whom they had seen going in and out of court for years under the Islamic Republic, be recognized in this way showed them that the world watched and appreciated their efforts. Most of the time they were struggling alone, but history was also watching them.

Because my position allowed me to travel around the region, I saw how special this was. No other Middle Eastern country had anything quite like it. Much of the region was still enamored with political Islam, and in countries like Saudi Arabia, many women were simply not interested in mounting an open challenge to the state's patriarchy. So in this, Iran was very special and ahead of its neighbors, and the movement had managed to flourish, despite Ahmadinejad's emergence.

"Your idea is tremendous," I said. "It is impressive and bold, and well conceived. I just think you have to be careful to direct it in a way so that it has maximum appeal. It needs to be an initiative that traditional and religious people also find themselves drawn to, not just the secularists."

The two nodded in agreement, but they said they had to discuss this aspect of their outreach with the committee charged with launching the campaign. Everyone had to support the group's key ideas before they could be adapted. I was pleased to see how naturally democratic the activists were in organizing and planning their initiatives, and that they were not prepared to accept something without consulting with their colleagues. I wished them the best of luck, and I said I looked forward to their launch.

The following week, Parvin and Noushin returned and showed me a draft of their One Million Signatures campaign handbook and introduction, which the group's legal committee had drafted. I made a few minor changes to ensure that all the content was consistently defensible in any court of law. After that, a date was set for the launch of the campaign: August 27.

What discriminatory laws, Parvin asked, should they start with? Divorce law and polygamy? Inheritance and child custody? I said their campaign should have only one objective—namely, the reform of all discriminatory laws. They asked if such an objective could be achieved under the Islamic Republic system.

I told them, "This must be the aspiration, the ideal. An ideal is like the sun in the sky. Perhaps no one can ever reach the sun, but you shouldn't forget that it's there. As to which set of laws you should start with, I think this is something you'd best ask the signatories."

When it came to launching the campaign, the authorities refused the women a legal permit to hold their meeting in a public place or assembly hall. So they had no choice but to start the campaign from the office of one of the group's supporters. The plan was to hold a brief ceremony and announce the campaign's objectives. But two hours before the start of the meeting, security officials warned the owner of the office building that such a meeting should not go ahead.

There was no time to inform all the participants. Everyone gradually began to arrive, and they faced a locked door. Noushin and Parvin were standing there, arms crossed over their chests, absolutely furious. Others looked anxiously at the security forces, who were now standing at the entrance to the street. Gradually those who had been invited to the meeting began to arrive, forming a large crowd in the street. I spotted a few journalists, as well, in the crowd.

Suddenly, a young girl shouted from among the crowd: "You can't stop us! The campaign will begin here . . . right in the middle of this street!" The crowd broke into applause at her suggestion, and the organizers began distributing sheets of paper for everyone to sign. An hour later, the crowd dispersed, and the security forces left as well, probably thinking that they had successfully prevented the meeting.

The following month, while on a visit to the United States to attend a seminar along with Desmond Tutu, the Dalai Lama, and all the women winners of the Nobel Peace Prize, I passed out the campaign's petition paper and asked everyone to sign it. Soon the media announced that all these prominent figures had come out in support of this action by Iranian women.

Though the organizers called their effort the One Million Signatures campaign, the key goal was never to simply collect signatures. The main objective was to raise awareness across Iran about discriminatory laws and to propel a wider debate around how those laws could be updated or changed. The campaign, which had both men and women in its ranks, used the meeting point of a signature collection as an occasion to speak to people and to emphasize the peacefulness of their work. Campaigners visited government offices and organizations, and they asked people for signatures at metro and bus stations. They organized street-theater events, visited women in their homes, and fanned out across the country. They found support and expanded quickly from Tehran to a number of other cities. There, activists from Tehran held "train the trainer" sessions, and these local activists began doing in all these cities what the key founders had started in Tehran.

What this proved was something deeply distressing to the authorities: that the demand for legal reform extended to women across the country, across class, geography, and social background. The campaign's great success was to develop and build women's awareness around key legal issues like equitable inheritance rights and inflation adjustment for dowries—these were areas that had the support of traditional and more secular-minded women alike, and the mounting pressure, plus the many thousands of accumulating signatures, made the state deeply nervous.

It was at around that time that the arrests began. Across the country, the authorities began going after activists, from senior leaders to even occasional participants. The chief prosecutor accused them of "conspiracy against national security" and the "dissemination of lies" in society. This was because after the officials had carefully scrutinized the handbook, the introduction, and all the material published and distributed by the campaign, they could not find even a single sentence that contravened an accepted tenet of Islam. This meant it would be impossible for the state to level charges of antagonism against Islam; there was not even enough to get a cleric who was on the state's payroll to declare that the activists were apostates. I had been watching out for this from the beginning. From that day at my office when Noushin and Parvin had brought over the campaign's draft documents, I had read them with an eye to what I suspected would someday happen.

When the activists went to court, I represented a number of them as their defense lawyer. In one of the trials, I openly challenged the state's claim that the women's work had somehow undermined national security.

"So a woman says she does not want her husband to have a second wife, and she refused to share her marital bed with another woman. Can you please explain to me how this will lead to Israel attacking Iran?" I asked the judge. He was not a cleric, but he had the required stubble and continuously played with a string of amber prayer beads.

The accusations were completely irrelevant and laughable. But with a justice system that had long ago lost its independence, that now walked in step with the

whims of a higher, repressive authority, the fact that
there was a court process meant very little. The judiciary sentenced both Noushin and Parvin to three years
in prison, and a number of others also received con-
victions. Many who avoided prison found themselves
later so harassed and vulnerable that they ended up
leaving the country.

Despite this, I consider their work a success. New
organizers continued to carry on their work, and kept
on collecting signatures. The campaign transformed
legal discrimination into a national social debate. The
social aspect is key here, because the feminist activists
managed to disentangle the women's question from the
high politics of East versus West, Iran versus the world,
and the Islamic Republic versus democracy. Topics like
equal access to education for women, blood money,
and polygamy became issues that ordinary women were
engaged with, and as a result, in the elections to come
they figured as a central part of candidates' campaign
pledges.

There were some small legal victories as well. In
2008, the campaign pressured the parliament into
amending the country's inheritance laws, ensuring that
women could inherit their deceased husband's properties. That same year, the parliament also granted
women the right to equal blood money in accidents
covered by insurance companies. Members of parliament managed to block Articles 23 and 25 of the "Family Protection" bill the Ahmadinejad government had
proposed in 2007, which would have enabled men to

take additional wives without their first wife's consent and would have mandated that women pay a tax on their fiancé's *mehrieh* (dowry gift). None of this meant that Iran's lawmakers were suddenly liberal and concerned with women standing equally before the law, but they were sensitive enough to public opinion to see that society itself was growing more progressive. And, as is often the case in Iran, Iranians managed to either nudge the regime ahead or pull it along with them—I'm not sure which.

CHAPTER 7

Spies on the Doorstep

♦

On an inky Tehran night in 2007, just before one in the morning, my old friend Haleh Esfandiari, an Iranian-American Middle East scholar at the Woodrow Wilson International Center for Scholars in Washington, D.C., was riding in a taxi along the Tehran-Qom highway, en route to Imam Khomeini airport. Haleh visited Iran two or three times each year to see her mother, an Austrian woman who had lived in the country for decades and was devoted enough to Iran that she stayed on there even after her Iranian husband, Haleh's father, passed away. As Haleh's taxi sped through the night, a car in the next lane started driving precariously close. It veered near, drifted away, then veered close again. Haleh clutched the door handle and shouted to the driver. He nervously slowed down, waving a hand at the other driver as if to say, *Are you trying to kill us all?* The car kept pushing closer and closer, until it edged the taxi onto the shoulder, forcing it to stop. Under the sickly orange glow of the streetlamps, two men jumped out and forced the doors of the taxi open. They grabbed Haleh's handbag and luggage, hopped back into their car, and sped off into the night.

A shaken Haleh, who couldn't fly because her Iranian passport had been in that stolen bag, returned to her mother's house and went to the police station in the morning to report the incident. The police referred her to some security officials, who, in turn, asked a few questions about her work, then let her go. She agreed to return a few days later and answer the rest of their questions. The next time she returned for more questioning, the agents arrested her. It now became clear that the motorway theft had been staged, an elaborate way to stop Haleh from traveling home to Washington.

Haleh's husband, Shaul Bakhash, a distinguished professor who taught at George Mason University and who, like Haleh, had been a noted journalist before the revolution, contacted me. Haleh was a grandmother and close to retirement, a delicate, petite woman whom no one could imagine in an Islamic Republic prison cell. He was distraught but composed, and he assured me that if I would agree to represent Haleh he would pay my fees, no matter how high. I explained to him that I had made a pledge to myself never to receive any payment from any political prisoner. Fulfilling that pledge was like performing a divine duty for me.

Should one receive money for fulfilling a divine obligation? He thanked me, and I started my work. But, as usual, the authorities did not permit me to visit Haleh; nor did they provide me with the case file to study. It was impossible to determine what the authorities believed to be the cause of her guilt. What had she been accused of doing? And why the staged highway robbery? Why had they not simply obtained an arrest warrant from the prosecutor and picked her up at home?

Defending such a client, under these circumstances, was a bit like being dropped into a spy film without any advance knowledge of the plot or even a sense of location. Often I felt as though I were rushing about in the darkness, banging on doors, searching for the elusive person who mattered, the individual who could reveal what was actually going on. In Haleh's case, the authorities blocked me from speaking to the interrogators who were seeing her regularly, and of course there was little question of my tracking down the intelligence officers handling her case, the ones who made all the decisions. Where would I even look for them? The precise location of the Ministry of Intelligence's headquarters in Tehran is still unknown to any but those who work there and those in the very highest level of the government. In all my interactions with agents, they had visited my office, keeping the place they returned to a secret.

There wasn't much I could do, but as I certainly needed to do something, I gave interviews about the case to the press, often hourly. I wrote a letter detailing the case to the U.N. High Commission on Human Rights—Iran was on the committee that year and I hoped it would release Haleh to save itself the embarrassment of having the issue raised during one of the committee's upcoming meetings. Not long after, the authorities released Haleh. Her friends and family in Washington had mounted an aggressive campaign in the Western media, pressuring the government for her release, and it had succeeded. She left Tehran and flew to Washington, D.C., never to return.

In the months and years that would follow Haleh's arrest, the Iranian state went on to arrest and detain other Iranian-American dual citizens. The policy was, first and foremost, designed by the state to create a bargaining chip with the United States. People like Haleh, and those who came after her, were effectively hostages, cases that American officials brought up through intermediaries and then directly with Iranian officials, in hopes of securing the release of American citizens. That it sought to create bargaining power through such means only highlighted Iran's desperation, as well as its willingness to use the most compromised means possible to achieve its political aims.

On a frigid winter morning, I was standing outside our apartment building, bundled in a warm woolen coat, waiting for a young colleague to pick me up. There was a light dusting of snow along all the spindly limbs of the trees, and the coffee-colored slush along the curb was

still frozen in patches. A few minutes earlier, my colleague had texted to say she was nearby, and so I had
locked up and gone outside, concerned that the ice and
snow on our street might give her trouble. Our street is
a tiny residential lane off the main thoroughfare in
Yusef Abad and, because of its slight angle, can be difficult to maneuver during wintertime. I might have
simply walked up to the main road and taken a taxi, but
by that time, the winter of 2007, I no longer went anywhere on my own. I had dispensed with my state-
appointed bodyguards, and during one of my recent
trips abroad I had bought a vial of pepper spray, which
I kept in my handbag. There was no particular threat
that compelled me to do this, just a general sense of
mounting tensions. I knew that the authorities were
increasingly displeased with me, and that sooner or
later they would choose some way of conveying that
more intensely. Sometimes, as when I was returning
home late in the evening or walking through a part of
Tehran I didn't know especially well, I clutched the
spray in my palm. I wasn't afraid of thieves; I was afraid
of spies.

I had recently received a legal summons to appear
before a judge and explain why I had shaken hands with
Jacques Chirac, the French president, the previous
year. Apparently some Iranian man had seen the hand-
shake on television or a photo of it in a newspaper and
had filed a legal complaint against me, arguing that by
shaking a man's hand publicly, I had brought shame on
him, this random individual, "before the entire world."

I had ignored the summons. I knew the state was desperate to put me on trial for something, but a complaint like this I simply refused to engage with.

It was becoming clear that Ahmadinejad's rise to power was inalterably changing everything. The political establishment was growing angrier and more intolerant, and the middlemen and loyalists Ahmadinejad had installed across the regime's many institutions were busy clanging shut any of the small, progressive openings Iran had experienced under President Khatami. The censorship authorities were aggressively stepping up their controls on what novelists, screenwriters, and academics could publish, and even books that had been vetted and published found themselves back on the censor's desk. *Girl with a Pearl Earring,* in its seventh print run, lost its publishing clearance, as did Gabriel García Márquez's *Memories of My Melancholy Whores,* which had been published in Persian under the already soaped title *Memories of My Melancholy Sweethearts.*

For activists and organizers, the situation was growing even more bleak, with state harassment of their families, threats from intelligence agents, and warnings of prosecution stepped up by the day. Worst of all was the narrowing of the space for public debate. Newspapers were becoming more bland in their coverage of politics, afraid of provoking the censors, and formerly outspoken academics and intellectuals were now more quiet. The vibrancy of Iran's political atmosphere, the very thing that made Iran so distinct in the region, was fading. In its place were arrests of journal-

ists and harassment of dissidents, and this put me in a
more fraught relationship with the state. Nevertheless,
I had no choice but to raise my voice and criticize the
government more publicly.

Finally a gray Peugeot slowed to a stop at the top of
our road. I waved to show I was coming and walked up
the sidewalk to greet my colleague. I was feeling rather
low that day, but I said nothing about that as we merged
in with the traffic and headed toward the Tehran revolutionary court.

Everyone who entered the court building had to go
through security, and as with all government buildings
and public places, there were special lines for men and
women. We walked toward the women's security section
and heard, from behind the curtains where the inspections took place, a booming voice chastising a woman
for allowing some locks of hair to show beneath her
head scarf.

"And what's this? Wipe it off," the voice said sharply.

"But it's just a bit of foundation—is it really a problem?" the other voice said softly.

"If you want to go in, it's a problem."

We waited until the woman behind the thick navy
curtain had fixed whatever was wrong with her appear-
ance, and then we went in. One of the security women
was sitting down looking at a magazine, and the other—
I could see instantly that it was she of the booming
voice—took up much of the small space. I remembered
her from my last visit to the court. She wore a severe
black *maghnaeh* that pinched at the skin around her

fleshy face, and her chador seemed to be worn over yet another black chador. Despite her girth, hardly any contour or flash of a figure was visible. She was clearly extremely religious. No deviation, no matter how minor, escaped this woman's stern gaze. Perfume, light-colored coats, things that scarcely any other security check would fault, that were probably not even technically infractions, made her mouth go tight.

But when bending close to pat me down, she whispered in my ear, "I respect what you do, to protect the rights of women. For the sake of Allah the almighty, please do something for the poor subjugated women. My son-in-law has taken a second wife, and he now wants to divorce my daughter. Everyone says he has used his legal rights. What kind of a right is this? Please, for God's sake, do something for women."

My colleague, who had been inspected lightly by the quiet woman with the magazine, had been waiting on the other side of the curtain.

"What took you so long?" she said curiously. "Did she hassle you?"

"No, not at all."

While the security guard's words had saddened me, they also bolstered me as I walked toward the court. The woman wanted justice for her daughter. Her words quietly echoed in my mind as we continued down the corridor, a reminder that the quest for justice was one that so many Iranians shared, regardless of their differences.

Because I was a repository for people's grievances,

because they sought me out to tell me their sorrows, I knew the security guard's concerns were just a glimpse into the vast, simmering dissatisfaction that ruled Iranian society. Government employees often confided their disappointments to me, in ministries and other offices I visited for work. Even judges sometimes complained openly to me, upset with some aspect of the status quo. Where did all that mistrust and resentment reside, I wondered. How could it just lie dormant inside so many people, as they went about their days, their multiple jobs, in this city choked with pollution, waiting and waiting for something to get better?

On another freezing cold winter day, a shoeshine man appeared out of nowhere and set himself up directly across the street from our apartment building. Our street is hardly wider than a car's width, and it dead-ends at a park. It is both entirely residential and not especially long, and the only people who ever venture down it are the very few who live there. It was clearly not a suitable place for a shoeshine man to try to make a living. Dressed in shabby gray trousers and a large overcoat, the man turned up every morning, sat on a wooden stool, and laid out his polish and brushes. The whole business was such a comic and blatant attempt by the security services to monitor me that the colleagues and friends who called at my office began making sarcastic comments to him as they passed.

"Business brisk these days, eh?" they would say.

"May you not be tired," one might add, using the common Persian phrase for greeting those one encounters in the course of work or labor. He would only smile politely, indifferent to these comments. I never saw him making notes, but he did have a mobile phone, which he used to report on the movements of those going into and out of my building. After a few weeks, he disappeared.

About a month later, walking up to the main road to buy cake from our local bakery, I saw that a freshly painted new newspaper kiosk had opened up at the top of our lane. It was carefully situated to give the kiosk owner a wide view of any cars or pedestrians heading down our street. As I walked past, I looked the man tending the kiosk straight in the face.

Less than a hundred yards away, there was another newspaper kiosk that had served the neighborhood for two decades. The owner's business was thriving, he sold nearly all the papers and magazines published in Tehran, and he was friendly and beloved by the whole area. All the neighbors and local shop owners suspected that the recently arrived newspaper seller was an intelligence agent, installed there by the authorities to, like the shoe shiner, monitor the comings and goings from my office. Although the authorities handled their surveillance so crudely that my neighbors and friends made jokes, it unnerved me to think that vulnerable families of detainees, potential clients, and activists already sentenced and out on furlough would come to meet me imagining that they were going to a private meeting when, in fact, their faces and identities would quickly be recorded and uploaded to the state's security bodies.

One afternoon, a client who had spent some time in prison for a political crime arrived for a visit. He slowly set his coat and umbrella down on a chair by the door, a grave expression on his face. Then he told me, "When I was just walking past the kiosk, I saw one of the revolutionary court's interrogators. He was inside, talking to the newsagent. I would remember his face anywhere."

That was when I knew without a doubt that my suspicions had been correct. I was being watched every time I entered and left my home. An intelligence agent was keeping vigil, with no other purpose than to watch me and report.

CHAPTER 8

A Fatwa to Defend

◆

As the Tehran winter turned to spring and the snow melted off the tops of the Alborz Mountains, the political situation continued to darken. Around this time, the authorities forced Javad to retire. After thirty years of service he was technically eligible for retirement, but he had had no plans to do so. He was energetic, in perfect health, and enjoyed his work as a senior engineer, and he would likely have kept working another five or ten years before applying for retirement. But one day the human resources officer of the engineering firm he worked for summoned him and said they were granting him retirement, effective immediately. The HR manager told him that the Ministry of Intelligence had indirectly made it known to them that this was because of my activities.

Javad wasn't devastated, but he was not exactly

pleased, either. There was still the possibility of working as a consultant—this didn't have to be the end of his
professional life—but I nevertheless felt a deep sadness
and guilt. My work had effectively ruined his. It was
another instance of his life being altered because of the
path I had chosen, another compromise that he tolerated with grace. Trying to make it up to him, I planned
a trip for us to Russia. But Javad's life changed after
that. He pursued a partnership that never panned out,
and he ended up putting work aside sooner than he
would ever have otherwise. It was an early sign that the
state would not permit us to flourish together.

I was sitting at my desk with my first morning cup of tea
when my buzzer rang. The authorities in Tehran had
recently rounded up seven leaders of the Baha'i faith,
and the community was shaken to its core. Iran makes
life difficult for the religious minorities it does accept—
Christians, Jews, and Sunni Muslims. But the Baha'is,
considered heretics by the Islamic Republic, are sin-
gled out for full-scale persecution. The Baha'i faith
emerged in Iran about two hundred years ago, founded
by the prophet Baha'u'llah. Today Baha'is number
around five million globally, with 350,000, a sizable
community, living in Iran as the country's largest single
religious minority. The Islamic Republic not only re-
jects the Baha'i faith but prevents Baha'is from holding
government jobs, denies them licenses for running
businesses like restaurants and hair salons, and forbids

their young people to study at universities. Since 1979, the state has executed more than two hundred Baha'is simply for their religious beliefs.

When the community leaders were arrested, no lawyer dared take on their case. In the legal realm, the Baha'is are the no-man's-land of the Islamic Republic. No one, even lawyers who represent feminists and democracy activists, will take on Baha'i cases, because the state's hatred and extreme sensitivity are so entrenched that the consequences, lawyers fear, will be too dangerous. That is why the families of those arrested came to me, and I agreed to act as their attorney.

Not long after I had accepted their case, a number of hard-line websites began reporting that my daughter Nargess had converted to Bahaism. Under the Islamic Republic's strict interpretation of Islamic law, converting out of Islam amounts to apostasy, which is punishable by death. It was a prelude to what, I imagined, would be further reports alleging my own conversion. They were trying to scare me into dropping the case, perhaps laying out some sort of trap.

I knew I was treading on dangerous ground and would have to think creatively. I contacted Grand Ayatollah Hossein Ali Montazeri, a senior cleric who had once been Khomeini's heir but had been cast aside in the late 1980s when he protested the regime's mass executions of dissidents. Since then, Montazeri had evolved into one of Iran's most liberal clerics, though the regime harassed him intensely and kept him under virtual house arrest. I wrote a religious query to Montazeri, asking openly whether Islam would permit a Muslim to defend a Baha'i accused of espionage. In response, the ayatollah issued a fatwa that said it was indeed permissible. The fatwa went so far as to specify that if one was certain that the accused Baha'i was innocent, then not only was it permissible to defend that person but it was *vajeb,* duty.

The prosecutor had said that the defendants could not meet with their lawyers until the end of the investigations; furthermore, I was not permitted to study the files or have access to the allegations against them. I went repeatedly to see the lead investigator in order to get some news about my clients, but he deflected all my inquiries. During one visit, he grew exasperated.

"You're a Muslim. How can you be defending a Baha'i?"

"It's precisely because I'm a Muslim and not a Baha'i that I want to defend them. I believe in freedom of religion, and Islam defends that right."

He looked at me stonily, so I felt emboldened to continue.

"Has the Koran not said, 'Oh Muhammad, tell the infidels: I do not worship your God and you do not worship mine. So, keep your religion for yourself, and I will keep my religion for myself too.' So what is the meaning of this Koranic verse?"

"It's a pity that the law does not allow it. If the law permitted me, I wouldn't show mercy even to their children. They are misleading our youths."

After about a year, my clients were finally permitted

to receive visits from their families, but they were still not allowed to meet with me. The relatives who were permitted visits passed me news. They told me that the security officials, including the lead investigator, had promised to show them leniency in court if they agreed to fire me as their lawyer.

My clients did not agree, and after they lingered in prison for another few months, I was finally allowed to study the case files. The prosecutor had accused them of spying for America and Israel and conspiring against national security. But their files did not contain any evidence or even reasoning that might point to their guilt. It was clear that they were being punished for their religious beliefs, but because it would cause such international condemnation to prosecute them on these grounds, the state had leveled espionage charges. Iranian criminal law does not formally consider being a Baha'i an offense, and because the courts had no evidence of spying, these Baha'is should have been released. But the Iranian court sentenced my clients, five men and two women, to twenty years in prison, where they remain to this day.

It was high summer, the whirring air conditioners of the neighborhood creating a collective hum that I could hear from my law office. I was reading an email from my daughter, absently sipping a sour cherry juice, and calculating the time difference with the East Coast in my head to see when I could call her. The rasp of my buzzer startled me. I wasn't expecting any callers, and I waited a moment before I got up to answer.

"Yes?"

"Mahdavi, from the Ministry of Intelligence. Do you have a moment?"

I leaned against the doorframe, wondering what to do. Mahdavi never came by without an appointment, and that afternoon I was alone. I reached for my head scarf and buzzed him in. When he entered, a second man followed behind.

"This is my colleague, Mr. Mahmudi. He will be taking over your file from me."

I knew Mahmudi wasn't his real name. He was in his mid-thirties, with light brown eyes, fair skin, and the requisite civil servant's pious stubble. His cologne reached me before he did; I imagined he must have applied it in the car before coming up. His eyes scanned my office with some disappointment, as though he had been expecting something far grander. His shoes were pointy, the style of working-class Iranians trying to appear urban and stylish.

"How are you doing?" Mahmudi asked, after I had made some tea.

"I'm very well, thank you." I had to remind myself to keep my arms uncrossed, so as not to appear discomfited.

"I'm here to talk about your activities. Maybe you can help us better understand exactly what it is you're up to. We thought you were mainly involved in human rights. But we see you're now providing reports to the United Nations. What's going on here?"

"Well, for one, we send our reports to several places," I answered. "But as I see it, there's nothing wrong with cooperating with the U.N., so there's not much to explain."

"It makes it political. Why don't you just do your reports and keep it at that?"

"If cooperating with the U.N. is so wrong, why is the Iranian government a member in the first place? And why does the Iranian Ministry of Foreign Affairs have such extensive dealings with the U.N.? Why do we even have an ambassador there?"

"I'm not here to talk about ambassadors," he said. "Tell me why you're also interfering in the election process. This is a political matter; it shouldn't be meddled with."

The Defenders of Human Rights Center had set up a committee to promote free and fair elections, based on the principles of an international body to which Iran belonged. The committee had assessed Iran's votes for two years and found numerous violations, which it had then passed on to the body itself, the Inter-Parliamentary Union. The Iranian government had not been pleased.

I tried to explain to my new monitor that we needed healthy elections to have a healthy democracy. I argued that otherwise people would grow dissatisfied and be compelled to stage another revolution.

Mahmudi listened to this impassively, drumming his fingers on the table. His eyes darkened as I mentioned the possibility of another revolution.

"Okay. So this National Peace Council you've set up. What's this? Your work has so many different branches," he said.

"Human rights are meaningless without peace. During times of conflict, or just a sense of impending conflict, it's nearly impossible to focus on rights like freedom of expression, or the right to an education. Everyone is just struggling to survive. So peace and rights are actually very connected."

"We're at peace now anyway, so it seems like wasted effort to me, at best," he said.

I didn't know how much further to go on. Should I really give a short lecture on human rights and their inalienable and existential meaning to an intelligence agent? He was demanding answers, and I had no other language in which to explain myself. He wanted to understand—or at least he was pretending to want to understand—how human rights and democracy and conflict prevention intersected, but such conversation demanded some sliver of a shared worldview, or, at a minimum, a shared understanding of those terms. He was getting antsy, pushing his chair back, as though to create more distance between us. I decided to simplify what I was saying and relate it to his work.

"I'm not interested in political power at all. That's not the aim of human rights work. I know that holds for my colleagues as well. We don't work with or for any opposition groups; we don't even particularly support one over the other. We're just committed to seeing people live freely and to making sure their legal rights are protected."

I described the various people who had joined the National Peace Council, how we had included film-makers and writers, scientists and doctors. We had set up the group during the presidency of George W. Bush, when his government spoke incessantly of war against Iran. All at once, he ran out of patience and interrupted me loudly:

"Kick all of these people out of your office. Don't let them back in again. Understood?"

"How can you say that? These are some of the most distinguished, prominent people in our society. I would never do that."

He made an exaggerated *pfft* sound. "These people you respect so much, they're simply nobodies. If you kick them out, they'll just melt and disappear like a snowball in the sun. They only feel strong because they're crowding under your umbrella."

In my head, I imagined saying, *And then you'll be happy? Then you'll leave me alone and let me do my work and stop monitoring and harassing me?*

But instead I took a curt tone: "Look, the center's office isn't mine. I've transferred ownership to the center as an endowment, and the board decides who should enter, not me."

"Do you have that endowment document handy?" he said, smiling with fake pleasantness.

"When you pray at dawn each day and when you fast

during Ramazan, do you get a receipt? Do you have documents that prove you fasted?" I was now raising my voice. "I've given that office to the center because in my belief system, human rights work is an act of worship."

At this he got up suddenly to leave. As he opened the door, he turned to face me. "*Inshallah,* we'll see you again soon."

The next day, I met with my colleagues at the center and told them about the meeting. They all agreed that I was protected by my international position as a Nobel laureate, that intelligence agents wouldn't dare take action against me, and that we should ignore their threats. So we continued with our work as before, taking on cases and spending long hours over coffee in the afternoon at our office, strategizing and planning for the future.

I made a point of finding out more about Mahmudi, the man who saw himself as my nemesis. I often thought of him, mulling over his single-minded purpose in bringing me down. Though he seemed to be the lead interrogator and agent handling the files of the country's most prominent dissident lawyers and activists, he was obsessed with me. I had never, in all my years defending people the state persecuted, come across another instance where one intelligence agent had dedicated his career to the ruining of a single individual. Mahmudi interrogated so many of my colleagues over the years, most often about me, probing them about what "Shirin" was up to, that I had gathered a picture of him in my mind. He wanted to know the most minute details of my life and behavior. He always referred to me as "Shirin" in his interrogations, to make me smaller, not worthy of being called *khanoum* or even by just my last name. He did it, I believe, to make it seem like he was intimate with me, that he was powerful and I was small.

He worked in the security branch of the Ministry of Intelligence, charged with the "security file," which concerned people like me: activists, critics, people seen as enemies. With his medium build and light brown hair, I took him for a fair Iranian of Azeri or Turkish background. He had been a militiaman since his youth, and those colleagues who could identify a regional accent down to the town said he was from Orumiyeh, in the Western Azerbaijan Province of Iran. It offended him to be called an interrogator; he thought this was too lowly a description for the work he did. He called himself a "case specialist" or, sometimes, an "intelligence officer." During interrogations he had a habit of mimicking people. " 'I want a lawyer,' " he'd say, inflecting his voice with his victim's cadence and manner of speech. " 'I want to call my family' " . . . " 'I'm just asking for my rights.' " He was married and had a daughter. I knew this because he paused one interrogation to take a call, speaking kindly to a little girl, promising to bring her something when he got home.

His obsession with me never abated. "You don't know how his eyes glitter with hate when he says your name," one of my colleagues related after undergoing several interrogations Mahmudi had dedicated to discovering details about me.

"Something about you enrages him personally," she went on. "It's as though you have something he wants badly. Social standing? Prestige? He's furious that you are who you are." Mahmudi was determined to bring me down, but at first, he started with small acts of sabotage.

On December 10, 2008, my organization had planned a celebration for the sixtieth anniversary of the Universal Declaration of Human Rights, the charter the U.N. General Assembly passed in 1948 in the wake of World War II, designed to enshrine the basic rights of individuals everywhere. About one hundred people were invited, and we had rented a tent, chairs, and heaters to make use of the office's large, tree-shaded terrace, to accommodate everyone. As we did each year, we would also present an award to a prominent Iranian activist who had worked for democracy and freedom of expression. That year, the award was going to Ezzatollah Sahabi, one of Iran's longest-serving activists, an advocate of political and citizens' rights, who was turning seventy-eight.

Our office secretary, a young Baha'i woman named Jinoos, arrived early to decorate the premises, setting up chairs and arranging flowers along with a few other colleagues. When I arrived at the center, I noticed dark Peugeots double-parked at the entrance. The front door to the building was wide open. I climbed the stairs quickly and found the door to the office also ajar. As I walked in, Jinoos said loudly, "Khanoum Ebadi has arrived."

Narges Mohammadi, one of my closest colleagues, a human rights activist in her late thirties whose journalist husband had spent much of the past decade in prison, came toward me. "Shirin, they've come to shut us down. They want us to leave now, so they can seal the entrance."

"What's happening? We're not doing anything wrong here!"

Two security agents dressed in dark suits stepped in from the corridor. "Regrettably, by order of the revolutionary court, we must close down this office immediately."

"Do you have a warrant from the prosecutor? Did you even have a warrant to enter the premises?"

"The door was open, and we just walked in. We have no warrant, but the prosecutor gave us verbal orders."

"I'm not accepting that." I moved to stand before the doors to the terrace.

The taller agent, who had an angry rash under his stubble, put a hand on his hip, where I knew he was concealing a weapon.

"We don't want any trouble, and we don't want to arrest anyone. But please be absolutely certain that this

ceremony will not be going ahead, under any conditions. We have to seal the office, and this is on highest
orders."

I knew he wasn't lying. In the Islamic Republic of
Iran, the orders of the Ministry of Intelligence and the
security apparatus always outweighed the law. I had
dealt with many cases where people resisted arrest or
challenged agents, demanding to see a warrant. Nearly
always they were badly beaten and dragged away, or
their office or home was ransacked. The officer standing in front of me with his hand on his gun was capable
of doing anything he wanted. He would never be rep-
rimanded, and he and I both knew it.

A third agent emerged from the back of the office
holding a video camera and started panning the room
with his lens. He videotaped the papers on the desks,
the photos on the walls, the fern in the corner, and
then turned his lens to all of our faces.

"Are you a film director? Just do your job and get
out of here," I said.

Jinoos pulled a camera we kept for witness testimony out of a desk drawer. Her eyes welled with angry
tears, and she wiped them with her sleeve as she
switched the device on and swiveled to face the agent
with the camera.

"Then I'm going to film you!" she said.

The agent looked dumbfounded and turned to the
lead officer, who had his back to the room, busy speaking
into a mobile phone, and hadn't noticed this exchange.

"Turn off that camera now!" the cameraman screamed, moving toward her.

"If filming is so bad, why are you doing it?" she said, pivoting to film all the agents in the room; there were now roughly a half dozen of them.

"Handcuff her!" the cameraman shouted, motioning to the other officers.

Whatever happened that afternoon, I didn't want Jinoos to get arrested. If she ended up at the police station, they would discover that she was a Baha'i, and she could end up spending years in prison.

"Jinoos, please stop," I said, putting my hand on her back. An agent stepped forward to take the camera, and she passed it to him. Her hands were trembling.

During this exchange, some of the guests had started trickling in. They looked around nervously, and one of them told us that a row of security officers were now standing outside the building, trying to prevent people from entering. We could hear shouting from outside, a man yelling, "It's over, we've put an end to it. Stand back!"

I rushed to the window and saw a swirl of bodies, women that I recognized as guests trying to move toward the doors. As the officers shoved them back, one woman, a director, stumbled backward and fell into the street. A man was waving his arms and objecting. An officer grabbed his arms, and another handcuffed them and pushed him into a waiting police car. The street was now entirely blocked with security cars.

The lead officer inside cleared his throat loudly. "Are you going to leave? We've asked you politely, but if you don't start to move, we'll throw you out." A few more officers entered the room, flanking the angry one who seemed to be in charge.

I fumbled in my purse for my mobile phone, to call the local police station.

When the commander answered, I said, "I need your help," feeling short of breath. "There are some men at my office, and they don't even have a warrant. They're trying to kick my colleagues and me out of our private property."

The officers were listening to my call, clearly furious. I pressed the phone to my ear, so that no one could overhear the station commander telling me that it was no use, asking me not to resist. "We will not help," he said. "This comes straight from the Ministry of Intelligence."

I looked at the officers, growing restless and impatient, striding about the office and shoving papers around desks. When I saw how white Jinoos's face was, I realized that putting up a fight would place her, the other young colleagues, and some of our guests in the most danger. They likely would not dare to arrest me. But what about everyone else? I waved Jinoos, Narges, and the others over to me.

"I know it's hard, but we have to go. There isn't any choice," I said, keeping my voice low. We walked around the office shutting off the computers, then stepped outside to turn off the heat lamps on the terrace. The pastries and cakes on the platters, the drinks, the decorations—we left it all there and filed out of the office, with the agents locking the door behind us. The guests outside had already been dispersed. It was approaching dusk, the shadows fading on the police cars that still lined the street. I wondered briefly whether anyone would show up tomorrow and find the doors bolted, or whether news would spread quickly among the city's activist and human rights community.

Because NGOs in Iran scarcely ever accepted foreign donations or funding—this would immediately compromise them in the eyes of the regime and lead to their closure—most functioned out of people's living rooms. The Defenders of Human Rights Center had been the only NGO with a big office, and it had become the gathering spot for numerous activists and organizers who worked on women's rights, the environment, and a number of other causes. It was a safe, social space where those building their society came together to debate and share news, often sitting under the trees on the spacious terrace, smoking and talking. Many called that terrace the "human rights canteen." So the shutting of the center meant more than simply closing down the physical space of a handful of human rights lawyers; it effectively closed down the main intellectual and social hub for those in Tehran working on civic activism. And perhaps that had been partly the objective. This thought made my limbs heavy with discouragement, and I looked up at the center's darkened windows, which reflected the neon sign of the bank on the ground floor.

I have always worked to build things in my country, to find ways to convey what human rights mean, to persuade people that they matter. It is simply in my character to do this, and I nearly always press on when things go wrong. But that evening, standing in the street before the officially bolted and sealed door of Iran's only human rights center, I allowed myself to think for a moment how hard it was.

Despite my efforts to keep Jinoos safe that evening, a week later the authorities discovered that she was a Baha'i and arrested her at her home. The authorities detained her for about a year, and sometime after her release, they imprisoned her father, for no reason other than his faith.

We also had smaller worries to contend with. All the equipment we had brought in for the ceremony—the tent, the large outdoor heat lamps, the chairs—were still on the office's premises, and we would have to pay a daily fee for their rental. I tried to contact various authorities to unseal the doors, just so we could return the equipment. After giving me the runaround for two months, they finally let us in for an hour, long enough to remove everything. The authorities never made the case against the center public, never sent it to court, and never gave me access to the file, so I could see what wrongdoing had been alleged against us. The investigator said the evidence was classified and that it would only be divulged to the court, which, of course, was never consulted on the matter.

Not long after the authorities permitted us that one hour of access, I ran into the building's manager on the street. It was a blustery afternoon, the wind whipping the trash along the gutters, steam rising up from the pyramid of fava beans a street vendor was cooking next to the kiosk where I had stopped to buy a newspaper.

"Khanoum Ebadi, now that I see you, there's something I wanted to mention," the building manager said. "One night after they closed your office—it was around eight P.M., when I was going home to my apartment—I noticed two men opening the door to your office.

"I recognized them because they were the same men who had rented the apartment next door to you last year. They were hardly ever there, but I recognized them. I told them that the office had been sealed by government officials, that it wasn't their flat in the first place, and demanded to know why they were breaking the seal. They showed me government ID cards and said they were intelligence agents and had the right to enter. They told me not to mention to anyone that I had seen them. But I thought you should know."

"Thank you for telling me," I said slowly. We had always had a good relationship. He was a kind man, and now I appreciated his integrity all the more.

"I better be off," he said, waving goodbye as he headed quickly into the bustle of people doing their after-work shopping. I watched him disappear down the street, rooted to the spot, absorbing what he had said. It meant that for at least the last eight months, since that neighboring apartment had been leased, the Ministry of Intelligence had been operating right next door to us. They had likely installed listening devices, capturing hundreds of our private conversations, taking down the most intimate details of our meetings with clients. Realizing that just on the other side of the wall, all these months, had been a Ministry of Intelligence listening post made me angrier than I could have imagined. Not because they were eavesdropping, for I expected that. But because they had been right up against us, hearing and knowing exactly what we did. They knew that we were doing human rights work and not plotting the regime's overthrow. And they had still shut us down anyway.

CHAPTER 9

Besieged

♦

With the center formally shut down, or at least physically shut down, the authorities imagined they were putting a stop to our work. But we almost immediately began working out of my personal law office. It was not a terribly big space: two rooms and a central reception area. But we fit in more desks and carried on.

One afternoon, as we were seated around the wooden conference table discussing our cases, someone buzzed at the door. Two sour-faced men, probably in their late forties, in baggy navy trousers, stood outside.

"We're here from the tax office. We need to inspect the premises," one of them announced.

"Is this really necessary? Since when do tax officials come inspect people's offices?"

The so-called tax men presented a letter that stipu-
lated their permission to inspect my office.

"Very well, go ahead," I sighed. But they had what
was effectively a warrant. They searched every nook of
my office, to the contained dismay and amusement of
my colleagues, and then left. I wrote to the minister
of finance to complain but heard nothing back.

A week later, the two men—now clearly intelligence
agents posing as tax officials—came back. This time, as
they stood in the doorway they told me that they had a
letter from the finance minister authorizing them to
confiscate various documents for a thorough audit.

"I'm not letting you take away my files," I said.
"These are confidential legal documents, and they have
nothing to do with tax or accounting. People trust me,
they come to see me as a lawyer, and they share very
personal information. I can't let you have access to
that."

"Sorry, but we have a warrant from the court, too,"
the tall one said, pulling out another piece of paper.

"I'm sorry," I said firmly. "I have responsibilities to
my clients."

"Well, we can do whatever we want. You have no authority over us." And they proceeded to push their way
inside.

Once again, I rang the police station. "There are
thieves in my office," I said. "They're threatening me
and trying to take my files. Please come immediately!"

Within minutes the siren wailed down the street,
and two officers, including the station commander,

came bounding up to the door. When the commander saw and spoke to the two "tax" officials, he was angry.

"These are government officials! Why did you lie to me?"

"In my view, they're thieves. And I'll only allow them to take away files if you, as the police station commander, formally testify in the official procès-verbal of the event that they removed material from my office against my objections and protest."

He agreed. We compiled a procès-verbal, and the intelligence officers carried away two large cardboard boxes full of any documents that had drawn their attention. They also took my computer's hard drive. Of course, the tax audit was just an excuse. What they were looking for, what they were hoping to find amid all those papers documenting the abuse of critics of the regime, was some piece of paper that might prove I was a spy. That I had links with foreigners, and that some faraway government was funding my work; that every month, the American government deposited a check into some imaginary bank account, as payment for my defense of Iranian political prisoners.

For an entire month, I protested, giving interviews to every reporter I knew, making noise about the confiscation of my files. After that time, they sent a two-line letter saying that I could have them back.

The intimidation, the endless monitoring, the new ways the regime found to trip up my work and frighten me—they never ceased. It had been like this, to some extent, from the beginning, when I resumed work after the revolution. But it was impossible not to admit that it was getting increasingly intense. I noticed Javad becoming more cautious, always checking twice or three times in the evenings that our front door was double-locked. Was there more gray in his hair, or was I imagining that? Did he seem lost in thought more often as of late, tapping his pencil loudly against the newspaper in the evenings? Perhaps I should have talked to him about it, and asked how he was coping with the added anxiety. But while I felt the state circling ever closer, it was a reality I most often chose not to think about, in order to simply cope with the passing days.

After the center's secretary, Jinoos, went to prison, I hired another young woman, Hedieh. She was studying for her master's in sociology, and her English was strong. Three afternoons a week, she stopped by the office for a few hours and handled the various calls and emails that came for me from abroad. About a week after she started work, she called and told me that intelligence officials had stopped her outside the university and warned her not to work for me. She was a women's rights activist, not the sort of person quick to wilt at an encounter with security officials, and she had told them to leave her alone. They had cornered her on a street lined with bookshops and plane trees, not far from campus.

"I'm not doing anything illegal. And I need the money," she told them. They warned her that if she didn't quit, they would have her expelled from the university. When she related this to me, both of us concluded that they were bluffing.

But when she arrived that afternoon, I was surprised to see her walk in. It was not one of the days she worked. Her eyes were puffy from crying, and her nose was red. The dean of her faculty had summoned her to his office and said that she would not be permitted to defend her thesis if she continued to work for me.

"He said, 'Are jobs so scarce these days that you have to work for Ebadi?'"

I patted her hand and rose to pour some tea.

"My parents think I should quit. They say the university's expelled many students for less serious reasons. But it's so unfair. I'm happy here; I'm learning new things."

"You need to listen to your parents," I said gently. "As a student, you're vulnerable. But once you graduate, the agents won't have anything so easy to hang over you. You'll always be welcome to work here."

She looked at me gratefully and then, with some embarrassment, collected her things.

As she opened the door, her eyes welled up again. I squeezed her arm. "It's fine, *azizam*. There will be many chances to work together."

She was not the first, and neither would she be the last. In the past few months, she was the third secretary the security apparatus had bullied into quitting. Each time the routine was the same: some chance encounter on the street, general threats, then very specific ones.

Always they found the most vulnerable aspect of the young woman's life and shoved their fingers into it. With the master's student, it was expulsion. With the next secretary, a law graduate who was preparing to sit for the bar exam, they threatened to deny her license to practice law. She was feisty about it, assuring me, "They won't be able to pressure me!" But she also soon came by in tears, after receiving a letter from the Bar Association stating that her license had been blocked by the intelligence ministry. And to her I said the same thing I said to all of them:

"You should go. You need to think about your immediate future. Whenever you want, you can have your job back."

She, too, smiled gratefully and hugged me, her hair smelling of smog and fruity shampoo.

I fully sympathized with these young women, and I was determined to keep them out of harm's way. For my own purposes, however, I was beginning to feel quite frustrated. My knowledge of English and computers was not really adequate, and I needed someone to help me. But who could withstand the pressures of the intelligence and security officials? What use would it be to find someone new only to have her forced to resign after a month or two? How could I navigate a way out of this cycle? They wanted to paralyze me.

The Nobel Women's Initiative ended up saving me. I and the other female laureates who had banded together to found the group had become very close and kept in touch, sharing both progress and challenges we faced in our various countries. Jody Williams, who won the Nobel Peace Prize for her work on land mines, was the first to suggest that I should work with a secretary who didn't live in Iran at all. The group hired a young woman based in Washington, D.C., as my secretary, and the plan was for us to talk on the phone twice a day, so we could update each other on the work I needed.

It was a sound idea, but costly. I practiced pro bono law, and compared to the going rate in Iran, the salary of a secretary in the States was considerable. The NWI women graciously offered to cover the costs. And so began the long months where I would plan my days around walking to a public phone—I didn't want to call her on a landline or my mobile, which the authorities would be tapping—to ring Washington, D.C., eight and a half hours behind. To make things even more complicated, my secretary had a baby and didn't want the phone's bell to wake her up, so I had to plan my calls around both the time difference and the baby's naps. But I was willing to do it. I wanted to show the intelligence officials my strength, and to what lengths I was willing to go. I would get up at five in the morning and walk to a pay phone. They needed to understand that I would never give up.

I woke up to my phone ringing. I thought I was dreaming, that it was Negar, my daughter in America, calling.

Then I opened one eye and saw my mobile on the nightstand flashing. I grabbed the device and pulled it to my ear.

"Yes?"

I heard heavy breathing. "You stupid bitch, be careful. We're running out of patience with you."

I hung up and turned off the phone. They were furious. Every time they set a trap, I stepped out of it. I knew this explained the phone call. But as I stared at Javad's form beside me, his chest rising lightly, I felt my own chest constrict. *Look how close they can get to us,* I thought. *Even here, while we are sleeping in our beds.*

Perhaps I should have seen it coming, should have acknowledged to myself how the state's animosity toward me was mounting steadily. But at the time, I was deeply shocked by what happened next. At two P.M. one day in January 2009, a mob of men with beards, carrying posters and walkie-talkies, arrived on the street outside my office. I was bent over a file cabinet when I first heard the shouts. When I heard my name, I froze.

"Death to the American mercenary! Down with the enemies of the Islamic Republic! Death to the traitor Ebadi!"

There were so many voices, it sounded like a whole demonstration. I was too nervous to go to the window, so I locked the office door and fled to my home, upstairs. Javad was there, already by the window himself.

"They're carrying banners," he said grimly. "And there are more coming."

I sank down onto the sofa, gripping my mobile phone. The shouts kept swelling and rising. I ran into the kitchen, where a smaller window, covered by a thin lace curtain, looked out onto the street. There was something like a hundred men out there, a mix of ages. They wore dark colors and angry expressions, and one held a large pipe. Others had batons.

"I'm going to go close the inside door," said Javad, walking swiftly out of the apartment. Our building had a large metal internal door that could be shut from the inside. Rarely used, today it might save us.

Left alone, I thought of Javad down there, separated from the mob by a metal door, and jumped up. I had to do something. With trembling hands, I dialed the local police station.

"There are men outside shouting, attacking my building. I think they're here to kill me." The words spilled out of me, verbalizing the thought I hadn't allowed myself to think.

The officer began telling me that he would send a car over, but I couldn't hear what he said after that, because of the sounds of metal being hammered and glass shattering. Javad was back, and he said they had started hurling stones. We stood there together, side by side in our kitchen, watching below. Two men were using a metal bar to pry the sign for my law office off the building. Others had taken out cans of spray paint and were busy spraying—I could only imagine obscenities—across the walls of the building. The others threw more stones and shouted that I must die, that I had betrayed the country.

I saw a woman who was holding a child's hand start turning down the slope to our road, see the commotion, and turn back. A moment later a police car appeared, slowing as it approached the scene.

"Finally they've come," Javad said, pivoting to run back downstairs.

"Wait—where are you going?"

"The police are here now; I'm going to talk to them."

I watched from my spot at the window as Javad approached the two policemen, waving at the building. I was scared for him, my hands shaking as I pulled the curtain back even farther, and I thought for a second that I should follow him. I could see him growing more distraught. The policemen stood calmly, doing nothing to intervene.

Within a few minutes, Javad came back, furious. "Do you know what they said to me? They said, 'They'll just chant some slogans for a while and disperse themselves.' What about the damage? The hacked-off sign? The spray paint? I told them, 'This is terribly offensive, an attack.' They just smiled at me."

I suddenly realized that my colleagues' homes might also be targeted, and I quickly phoned two or three of the most prominent and warned them. I saw some of the neighbors start coming out of their buildings. One of them, an older man from two doors up, was holding a video camera and had started filming the assailants. It was so brave and unexpected that my throat caught. Within moments, one of the policemen—of the pair who had done nothing to prevent the attackers—went over and confiscated his camera.

The mob stayed on for another thirty minutes, their chants slowly deflating. Eventually they began walking off. They were members of one of the state's hard-line volunteer militias. Culled from the poorest strata of society, they were religious enough to be radicalized further in a militia's fold. These were the men the state dispatched when it wanted to brutalize dissidents, attack European embassies, raid feminist demonstrations, or otherwise bully Iranians yet keep itself distanced from that repression. By sending in the voluntary militias, the state maintained some measure of plausible deniability, and it often called the militiamen "students." Because of this setup, the militiamen who attacked our building were permitted by the police to wreak their havoc; this was why the police confiscated our neighbor's camera but not the thugs' cans of spray paint.

That evening, Javad and I stayed in, hovering around each other. I cooked chicken with barberries, in saffron and orange sauce, and we ate in silence, the sense of security we had always felt at home now gone. The ringing of my cellphone punctured much of our quiet evening. News about the attack had swiftly reached reporters, a number of whom showed up immediately, snapping photos of the damage, ringing our bell for a few quotes. What everyone who came down marveled at, apart from the extent of the damage itself, were the comic misspellings in the graffiti. The attackers had written "America crone" on the wall and had misspelled the Persian for "crone," *ajooz.* The irony here was that the state claimed that "students" had been responsible for the attack.

The news reports began reverberating internationally, enough so that two weeks later, the police officers who had merely observed the attack came to my office.

"Can you please get your building repainted?" one officer asked. "Every reporter coming to Iran now stops and photographs it. These reports are actually very damaging to your reputation, because these slogans on the walls make the foreign journalists think the Iranian people don't like you."

I laughed openly. "Whoever sprayed those slogans on my building can come back and clean them off themselves. I'm not doing a thing."

"But, Khanoum Ebadi, your reputation?"

"Don't worry about my reputation. The people understand very well who provoked and backed the attackers."

The defaced building walls remained as they were, the angry slogans bright red and glaring, for about three months. Then, one day, a few municipal workers came along with buckets of paint and began covering them up.

CHAPTER 10

A Mother's Test

♦

I was standing in the Tajrish bazaar purchasing vinegar when my mobile rang, flashing the number of a colleague from the Defenders of Human Rights Center.

"Omid Mirsayafi is dead," she told me. "They delivered the body to the family two hours ago, and they're saying it's a suicide."

The previous spring, the authorities had gone after Omidreza Mirsayafi, a young blogger from a working-class family who, like so many Iranians, was finding it harder and harder to get by. He had written an open letter to Supreme Leader Ali Khamenei on his blog, describing himself as a young Shia Muslim in need of help getting either a job or a loan, so that he could set up his own business. Would the supreme leader help him, he asked, just as Khamenei had helped the Lebanese?

Mirsayafi was referring to the outpouring of support Iran had extended to Lebanon in the wake of the Lebanese militant group Hezbollah's 2006 war with Israel. As Hezbollah's main supporter, Tehran sent hundreds of millions of dollars in aid and helped rebuild hospitals and homes in Beirut bombed during the war, bringing salaries and jobs to thousands of Lebanese. Like many young Iranians facing 30 percent unemployment, Mirsayafi had chafed at his government's priorities. The tone of the letter was polite, but it still provoked the anger of security officials, who filed a complaint against Mirsayafi to the judiciary, which then tried him and sentenced him to two and a half years in prison.

The judge ignored the fact that other than his letter of protest, he mainly wrote about Persian classical music, new songs he liked. He was sentimental and posted pictures of roses and poets until his imprisonment in the spring of 2008. Now he was dead.

"Meet me at the office in an hour. We'll go to the family," I said, handing the vinegar to the shop owner. I rushed back home, growing antsy as the taxi inched through the traffic, heavy because of Norouz, or the New Year, celebrated at the spring equinox. As I waited for my colleagues to arrive, I read through a selection of Omid's blog posts that we had saved on the office computer. Now that he was dead, his writing seemed eerily prescient.

In one post two years before he had written, "I have never been a person who would stoop to self-censoring and will never be. I'd rather not write at all if I have to stop being frank and honest in my words."

In another post he wrote about an experience that he called his second "birth," when something inside him compelled him to stop being a "passive bystander" in the face of committed wrongs. He described walking through a park in central Tehran on a day when young people were demonstrating in the streets.

> I was standing around one of the gates near a young married couple. A seventeen- or eighteen-year-old boy, clearly a religious extremist, approached us.
>
> "Beat it! Disperse!" he spat.
>
> We didn't pay any attention. The boy raced toward the young couple, addressing the young man: "Didn't you hear me, husband-of-a-whore? Didn't I just tell you to get the fuck out of here?"
>
> The young man was too shocked to give even the smallest hint of a reaction. Obviously he could not simply ignore the insult—yet if he did anything he was sure to get arrested. Having witnessed the scene up close, and without any second thought, I ran at the Basij [militia] boy and shoved him aside.

Omid went on to recount the other paramilitaries descending upon him with batons, beating him to the ground and dragging him into a police van. He spent twenty days in prison for that, and writes that he came out a "different Omidreza." He said, "I learned that you create yourself."

I was immersed in his thoughts, so gentle and yet so uncompromising, when my colleagues arrived. It took us over an hour to reach the family's neighborhood, which was across the city, tucked deep into the faded, sooty districts of Tehran's south. We finally found the house on a small side street lined with decaying tenement buildings. Omidreza's father opened the door. He was an older man, with gray stubble, dressed in modest, loose trousers and faded shoes. Their house was tiny, two stories, with each floor a single, small room. The male relatives were seated on the floor, on a worn carpet, looking down and trying not to cry. They greeted me and my colleagues. Three women of the family sat outside the doorway in the corridor, listening. The whole time I was there, I could hear the sound of their weeping.

They were all working-class men, and they spoke timidly to us, the lawyers who had traveled down from the north to pay condolences for their boy. One of the men, who may have been Omidreza's uncle, felt more comfortable speaking and led the conversation.

"He was the calmest boy. Always reflective, always asking questions. We know he didn't kill himself. He would never do such a thing. We know they tortured him, and we want to complain."

"Has there been an autopsy?" I asked.

They all looked at me blankly, then shook their heads.

"But why not? Why didn't you have one done?" I realized from their blank faces that they didn't know what an autopsy was. "If the forensic doctor had examined him, there would have been evidence of the torture."

"The ones who washed his body before burial, they saw all the bruises. They saw blood around his ear and head. They can be witnesses," the father said. His hands, brown and rough and lined, were folded limply in his lap.

I explained that such testimony wouldn't hold in court, that sometimes bruising can come after death, depending on how the corpse is handled, and that only a formal autopsy could prove torture. But an autopsy would have required the permission of a judge, which would certainly not have been granted; and even in many cases, I explained, where we had had forensic evidence of torture, we had been unable to secure a conviction. I didn't want this devastated family to go through any more than they already had, to pursue a legal battle that would produce only more heartbreak and anger. I tried to soothe them in terms they could understand, explaining why legally we had so little recourse. Fortunately, they were religious and could perhaps reconcile what had happened to Omidreza through their faith.

"In another world, justice will be served. When justice is not available to us in this world, there is nothing for us to do but seek refuge in a higher power," I said.

The family thanked us and rose to see us to the door.

As I passed the corridor, Omid's mother pressed my hand; her eyes looked hollowed out, her skin as pale as her white chador.

Is there anything more unnatural in this world than losing a child? And then to trust that justice must be forfeited to God? This was always the most painful part of my work: the searching eyes of the mothers and fathers whose children had been killed or were imprisoned, seeing in me some potential help. But the reality is that the fate of their sons and daughters rests largely on the political conditions of Iran, not on my abilities as a lawyer. When there was nothing I could do, I resorted to words and tea. My colleagues called my approach "tea therapy," because when these families came to my office, I usually brewed a pot of tea. And as we sat together drinking, I tried to talk about different things. I recounted the problems other families in similar situations were facing. Just so they would know they were not alone, that others were in a similar place, suffering alongside them. Sometimes this eased their despair by a shade. When they left my office, they often seemed calmer. When I couldn't reduce the burden of a family through my work, I could at least try to soothe their pain.

One afternoon I was in my office working quickly, trying to clear the files off my desk so that I wouldn't have to take them upstairs with me in the evening. My daughter Nargess, now living in Canada while studying for a master's degree in law, was returning to Tehran that evening to visit with us and finish up some loose ends with her law apprenticeship. I had put some lamb out in the kitchen and had left the rice to soak. Because I was rushing to get upstairs, I had been drinking more tea than usual all day, and when I felt my pulse racing a bit, I chalked it up to too many cups.

Javad was not yet back, and I was alone when I went upstairs. I moved about the kitchen, listening to the radio while chopping herbs, mixing yogurt, setting out pickles—arranging all the numerous elements required of a proper Persian dinner. Javad rang to say he was downstairs, and I grabbed my manteau and head scarf to head to the airport.

I tried to chat naturally as we drove and went inside, but once I saw Nargess's face as she emerged from the arrivals hall, I knew something was wrong.

"*Maman,* they've taken my passport away," she said.

"Who took it? What did they say?"

"A security officer. At passport control they asked me to wait, and then a security officer came and took it away. He didn't explain why, and when I demanded to know, he said I would receive a letter calling me to the intelligence ministry for investigation. He said they would explain the allegations against me there."

"We'll talk about it in the car," I said, putting my arm around her.

Noticing how grave her father and I looked, she stopped in the parking lot.

"I'm actually fine, you know. I told them maybe they

were doing me a favor. Maybe I won't have to start my PhD in the fall after all."

I was struck by this. When had she become so unflappable, able to be breezy under interrogation with an intelligence agent who had just confiscated her passport? We sometimes do not know our own children until life throws some unimaginable obstacle in their path and they respond with a courage we would never have had the opportunity to see otherwise.

The empty expanse of desert stretched before us on the Tehran-Qom highway, only the billboards lit up as we sped back toward the city. I tried to match Nargess's high spirits, but when we arrived home, I sent her off to take a shower and stood in the kitchen, thinking.

I felt as though it had started. As I stared at the old wooden clock on the wall, which I had bought on Jordan Street not long after our marriage, I couldn't say what, exactly; I couldn't follow the thought out to its logical progression. But it was clear enough. The state had finally started going after my family. It wasn't just content with me anymore. I had witnessed this over the years with many of my clients, dissidents and activists whose relatives suffered state intimidation, were hassled and threatened and sometimes blackmailed or imprisoned, all "collateral damage" in the quest to get the original target—the dissident or activist or journalist in question—to drop their activities. It was the dirtiest of the methods the security agencies used, exploiting these families and their emotional ties. In one typical tactic, the spymasters would simply arrest the loved one of a political prisoner who was resisting the state's demands to make a false confession and incriminate himself. They would then tell the prisoner that his sister or wife had been arrested, and that unless he confessed, they would be forced to torture her. It was all designed to identify that weak point, the point they could press on to exert their pressure.

But I wasn't an activist or an opposition figure. I was just a lawyer, by dint of having my career as a judge suspended—a lawyer working to make the laws of the country more fair, trying to promote lawfulness. To me this was as clear as the light of day, but for the authorities, growing more merciless by that same light, it seemed to make no difference. I called Nargess and Javad to dinner in the kitchen.

"It's a test," I said as we sat down around the table. "It's a test to see if I'll cave, if they can use Nargess to get to me. If we react, they will try to use her forever. But if I stand firm and don't respond, they'll realize they'll need another tactic."

Javad frowned at this. "So what do you suggest—that we do nothing?"

"Well, what can we do anyway? We can only show that we aren't shaken, that we know she hasn't done anything wrong, and that we'll proceed with our lives as usual. It's a game, Javad, to see who'll blink first."

He said nothing to this, moving the food around on his plate listlessly. He would clearly rather not be having the blinking contest at all. But Nargess's eyes glittered.

"I'll be fine, *maman*," she said. "I have no problem going to see them. I really haven't done anything wrong."

In the days that followed, I sometimes overheard her on the phone with her friends, still laughing off her situation.

"It's actually great to be stuck in Iran—I guess I'll have to spend the whole time at the Caspian, by the beach," she would say. Another time, what she said made me stifle a smile: "It's no bother at all. Finally, I'm becoming important!"

As a precaution, Javad insisted that we install a burglar alarm in our house. He chose a system that would automatically alert the local police station in case of a break-in. I found this ridiculous, because if we ever faced attack it would be the authorities themselves who would be responsible. But I saw that installing the alarm made Javad feel more secure, and I went along with it.

Several days passed, and the authorities summoned Nargess for questioning on the very day I was due to travel abroad for a seminar. My phones were tapped, my emails were read—all of this I knew. So it was evident that intelligence agents had timed their little game purposefully. Would I leave the country, knowing that my daughter was sitting in a government office with the officials of a ministry that just years prior had plotted my assassination? Would I board that plane and turn my back on my daughter, aware that so often when intelligence agents summon someone for "investigation," it is an occasion to arrest them? Would I blink?

"Nargess is a grown woman now; she's perfectly capable of defending herself. And I agreed to this conference ages ago—I really can't cancel at the last minute. If I were to drop my work every moment my children needed me, would I ever get anything done? Her father is here; they'll be fine." I said such things into the phone at every opportunity, several times a day, until the day of my departure and Nargess's interrogation. It felt strange to have scripted this conversation, to be saying these things into my home and office telephones while imagining the intelligence agents sitting across town, in some fluorescent-lit room, taking notes. Notes that would later go to higher security officials, who would be monitoring my reaction. Perhaps another mother, a mother whose work did not involve knowing and responding to the tactics of a highly trained security apparatus, would have thought me merciless.

But I understood that if I postponed my trip by even a single day, in order to ensure that Nargess came home safely and that her passport would be returned, they would spot my weakness. That would be the real danger. They would know then that they could use Nargess against me, and it was that I feared more than anything. If they concluded that she was my weakness, there would be no telling what they might do to her next, or to me. And so while it was one of the hardest things I have ever had to do in my life, I said goodbye to Nargess and Javad that morning in the living room, kissed them both, and then drove to the airport to board my flight.

When I landed in the United States, I immediately called home. Javad told me that when Nargess turned up for the appointment, the officials simply handed her passport back, without any investigation or questioning at all. So I had been right. I thanked God that if nothing else, all of my years of being watched by the security agencies, and defending clients permanently in their nets, had taught me enough about how they worked. To this very day, no one has explained to us why Nargess's passport was withheld after that trip, or what was being investigated. Nor has anyone explained why her passport was returned.

CHAPTER 11

The Farewell

◆

In the early spring of 2009, Iran began gearing up for
the June presidential election. Ahmadinejad's popularity had sunk abysmally; Iranians widely reviled him
for ruining the economy and for the repressiveness of
his rule: the stepped-up censorship, the morality police, the conservative Islamic agenda that seemed to
slowly, with each passing month, find a new quarter of
Iranian public life in which to assert itself. Because
Ahmadinejad's tenure had proved so disastrous for
such a wide swath of Iranians, the upcoming election
was emboldening people to express their frustration in
ways they might not have dared months prior. The students at Sharif University of Technology, in Tehran,
disrupted the president when he spoke on their campus, chanting, "Liar! Liar!" This was repeated at several of his public addresses.

The two key challengers to Ahmadinejad were Mir Hossein Mousavi, a former prime minister who had a reputation as a clean politician, and Mehdi Karroubi, a progressive cleric and former speaker of parliament. Both were determined to avoid competing directly with each other to prevent another Ahmadinejad term at any cost. Motivated, savvy young people manned their campaign headquarters. Former president Mohammad Khatami, the reformist who spent eight years moderating Iran before Ahmadinejad turned up, hung a green scarf around Mousavi's neck in a ceremony. It was a symbolic show of support from the still widely respected cleric, and green, the color of Islam, became the color of Mousavi's campaign.

In the weeks that followed, the streets of Tehran were full of green balloons and ribbons, with green flags flying from lampposts. The city was suddenly transformed from the sluggish, smog-choked capital of bitterness, people complaining about the rising cost of milk and meat, into an alert, excited citizenry discussing foreign and economic policy. Young people, especially, were so excited that they had taken to spending whole evenings and much of the night in the streets.

On the eve of the election I was in a taxi stopped at the intersection of Vali Asr Street and Vanak Square, in north-central Tehran. This was one of the busiest stretches of the long boulevard that slopes down from the Alborz Mountains to the south of the city, lined all the way with plane trees. Commissioned by an Iranian shah to rival the Champs-Élysées, Vali Asr was the stretch of Tehran where the children of the elite raced their Ferraris, where porticoed boutiques sold velvet curtains from Milan that cost more than a construction laborer made in a lifetime, where prostitutes loitered at rush hour, where taxi drivers and young men with long hair and grunge-rock T-shirts lined up to buy hot stew from curbside stands. The aspirations of Tehran's eight million citizens seemed to pulse here.

An accordion bus had stalled in front of my taxi, and the street was loud with the mad honking of traffic. But instead of the usual children selling matches and threaded orange blossoms, young people in bright green headbands were winding their way around the stationary cars. They were leaning into windows to pass out flyers and campaign posters bearing the photo and green banner of their candidate in the next day's presidential election.

A few approached my taxi, and as they came closer, they recognized me.

"It's Mrs. Ebadi!" cried a young man with heavy glasses and a green scarf. "Who are you going to vote for?"

Although the taxi window was closed, he was shouting so loudly that I could hear him clearly over the car engines and the radio. I lowered the window to reply, but a young woman waved a green balloon and answered for me:

"Of course she's going to vote for Mir Hossein!"

I extended my hand and took the campaign leaflets and flyers. "I'm voting for freedom," I said.

By now a small crowd had gathered around my taxi, everyone talking and laughing together. They had all heard me, and they interpreted my response as support for their candidate.

"That means she's going to vote for Mousavi," said the young man with the scarf. "Mousavi is the one who—"

"No, didn't you hear her? Freedom is with Karroubi," another interrupted, holding his posters aloft.

I laughed at their back-and-forth and was about to say something when the taxi started to move. I turned to wave as they stepped back onto the sidewalk, their arms filled with leaflets. It had been a long time since I had seen young people in Tehran animated in this way, talking politics freely on the street as though they felt themselves to be citizens of a country that gave them the right.

It took me another half hour to get home. I unlocked the door to my law office and hurried to make tea ahead of my colleagues' arrival. I wondered, with the election taking place in the morning, whether the authorities would pay much attention to the report my colleagues and I would be releasing later in the week. I printed out and stapled copies of the draft report and our meeting agenda, keeping an eye on the clock. In the past, I'd had an assistant to help me with such tasks, but the authorities had recently arrested the last young woman who'd worked for me. Now I mostly managed on my own, aware of the risks anyone who worked with me had to take. I stopped for a moment to catch my breath, and remembered to take out my mobile phone and remove the battery. I did not want the authorities to spy on our meeting.

It was dark by the time my four colleagues from the Defenders of Human Rights Center arrived. Since the authorities closed our office in December 2008, we were still holding our weekly meetings at my law office. Our caseload defending arrested activists and journalists had doubled in the past year, as the state intensified its crackdown on its critics. Despite the arrests of a number of my colleagues and increasing harassment, we were persisting with our work, and all of us hoped that this election would bring a president into office who would tolerate our activities.

That evening we were meant to be working on a report about underage executions, one of the gravest flaws in the country's justice system. Though the report was important, everyone was caught up in the excitement of the election. Around the conference table, none of us could concentrate; we just wanted to discuss the presidential election.

The outcome mattered dearly to all of us. If Mahmoud Ahmadinejad was elected for a second term, the country would slide even more deeply into repression. Ahmadinejad would certainly not allow the center's office to reopen, and there would be more censorship, more arrests of activists, a more suffocating political climate than what we were already struggling to cope with. But if one of his opponents, either Mir Hossein Mousavi, the candidate of the young people who had stopped my taxi, or Mehdi Karroubi, the moderate cleric, won, there would be a decent chance of the atmosphere becoming more relaxed. Newspapers could again offer a platform for debate, and all the marginalized reformists who had been pushed out of public life could edge their way back into politics. I was not anticipating a freewheeling democracy, just a return to the competitive politics and lively press that had predated Ahmadinejad. Most important, I hoped we could resume our human rights work more freely.

We gave up discussing the report and talked about how our various neighborhoods had come alive in anticipation of the vote. "In my apartment block, there were young people up until three in the morning shouting, 'Ahmadi, bye-bye! Ahmadi, bye-bye!'" said Narges Mohammadi.

Others in the group recounted similar stories from across the city. One of the lawyers said that a group of young people had stopped her on a street corner and invited her to join a political discussion about how to end Iran's international isolation. Another said she'd been struck by how respectful everyone was during these heated discussions, in bakeries, in traffic, at newspaper kiosks. After discussing all that we had seen around the city, we felt that the momentum was clearly against Ahmadinejad and there was little chance that he would be reelected. Virtually everywhere in Tehran, from the working-class districts at the city's outskirts to the middle-class areas of the center and the north, Iranians were visibly shifting toward the progressive candidates. We had worked for so long now without any prospect of change, and this new, delicate hope made our efforts seem more urgent than ever.

Suddenly Narges clapped her hands and yelled, "Why are we wasting time? This report is supposed be published in a week!"

Everyone went quiet, and we bent our heads down, sipped tea, and began to work. It took us a couple of hours to finish, and we agreed to meet again the next week, upon my return from a short trip to Majorca, where I was heading that evening to deliver a speech on freedom of expression. My colleagues said goodbye and headed off into the night. I washed the teacups, tidied the office, and went home upstairs.

Javad was sitting on the couch watching television, waiting for me. "What took you so long? I was hoping you'd get back a bit earlier before you have to leave again."

He was right. Since our younger daughter, Nargess, had moved abroad two years earlier for graduate study, I'd been working longer hours, and his complaints, though rare, were fair. I sank down beside him on the couch and leaned lightly against his shoulder. "I'm sorry—we got caught up talking about the election. But this is my last trip before the summer, and then we'll have three months to ourselves. With Nargess, too." This summer, our daughter would be coming home from The Hague, where she was apprenticing after having finished her master's in Canada, and I was looking forward to the break. We would go to our orchard cottage in the countryside just beyond Tehran, invite our relatives to visit, and eat our lunches outside, in the sun.

I started washing some lettuce for a salad, then set the table for dinner. We were eating when my cousin from Germany phoned to say he would be arriving in Tehran in a couple of days. I invited him to spend time with us at the orchard. I thought about asking my brother and sister as well, and the idea of this family gathering cheered me up as I packed my bags for the airport. I was shoving some clothes into my carry-on bag when Javad brought me a cup of tea. "Just stop for a minute and relax before you leave."

At that moment I loved my husband as much as any-time in our nearly thirty-four-year marriage. He was perpetually worried about my health, chiding me to eat less rice and to get more exercise. He paid attention out of concern, but he never nagged, like a true part-ner. He had been this way from the very beginning: in the early years of my judgeship, he never expected me to entertain or make my own jam, like a good Iranian housewife, and in the following years, he took care of the girls when I had to travel abroad for work.

The doorbell rang. It was the driver who would be taking me to the airport for the overnight flight. I picked up my bag and scanned the room, in case I was forgetting something. By the front door Javad stood waiting for me, as he always did, holding my mother's Koran. He smiled gently and held it high, so that I could pass under it, as is Iranian custom, so that it would protect and safeguard me during my trip. I passed under the holy book three times, bent my head down to kiss its cover, and then turned to hug Javad.

"Come back quickly," he said, squeezing my arm. I walked downstairs to the waiting taxi, still feeling the warmth of his hand on my back. Little did I know that I would never see my home, or my country, again.

CHAPTER 12

The Stolen Election

♦

It was really only my body that arrived in Majorca; my head was back in Tehran. The moment I entered my hotel room, I switched on my computer. The news sites were reporting a massive turnout at polling stations. Only significant turnout could defeat Ahmadinejad and his fundamentalist allies.

The next day I was sitting in a café on a cobblestoned alley in the old town of Palma with my Persian-Spanish interpreter, Rima, and some other organizers. Rima checked her phone and then shouted happily, "Mousavi has won!" But in the time it took to explain to those with us what had happened, and accept their congratulations, another email arrived.

Rima read from it dully: "Ahmadinejad has won in the first round, with a sweep of twenty-four million votes."

I looked quickly at my watch, carefully calculating the time difference. How was it that the votes had been counted so quickly? And twenty-four million, such an enormous margin? Where had his supporters been during those final days? What of the votes of all the young people who had thronged the city? I felt a lead-enness come over me, as the implication of this—that the center would be closed for at least another four years—sank in. I apologized to the group in the café and returned to my laptop at the hotel, where I spent the next several hours. Karroubi and Mousavi were object-ing to the vote, alleging fraud. The results had Kar-roubi at only 300,000 votes, a number he charged was less than the total number in his political party and campaign headquarters. Mousavi leveled his own ob-jections. There was talk of tampered boxes, of the un-seemly haste in which the vote had been announced, the astonishing returns that showed that each reformist candidate had failed to carry even his own hometown—unthinkable. Words like "stolen" were now being used, and shocked crowds were gathering. I spent the whole evening on the phone, talking to relatives, to col-leagues.

The next day, when I woke up, I learned that the supreme leader had sent a message of congratulations to Ahmadinejad; this sealed everything. It meant that the objections of the moderates would be ignored. Crowds gathered outside the Interior Ministry to again protest the result; officials came out and told them they would investigate. But it was clear that as far as the re-

gime was concerned, the vote was finished; now Iranians would just have to accept the result.

But this time they refused. On the night of June 13,
around midnight, the authorities began arresting people, among them the most distinguished politicians of
the land. They even arrested Dr. Ebrahim Yazdi, the
leader of the Freedom Movement, who was seventy-
eight years old and in the hospital, attached to IVs for
cancer treatment. They wheeled him away in his hospital bed and took him to prison.

That same night, close to three o'clock, a band of
Ahmadinejad's supporters, accompanied by the police,
attacked a University of Tehran student dormitory.
They shot five students dead and left at least one hundred wounded.

On June 15, millions of Iranians flooded the streets
of Tehran in the biggest demonstration since the 1979
Islamic Revolution. They marched peacefully and
largely in silence, holding up placards that read,
"Where is my vote?" and "Our silence is loud with what
we cannot say." They carried a green banner hundreds
of yards long, a sign of their support for Mousavi, who
himself came out to greet the crowds. He promised to
do something, to safeguard their votes. The immense
crowds around the city were peaceful, but in two inci-
dents authorities fired on protesters. At an arms depot,
they shot at least two young people. When the injured
were taken to the hospital, the authorities showed up
and carted them off to prison. The Ministry of Culture
and Islamic Guidance ordered all foreign journalists to

leave Iran; the authorities arrested a number of Iranian journalists and sent messages to others, saying that snipers were waiting to open fire on them, should they leave their homes.

My hotel room in Majorca, with its brightly patterned blue bedspread and lemon walls, felt like a cage. A few of my colleagues, I learned, had been arrested; others had received threats and had gone into hiding. At some point, the state had slowed down the Internet connection. With fewer and fewer emails coming through, I relied on the phone.

"Many think this is a coup. Don't come back to Tehran right now," said one colleague I managed to reach. "Wait at least a month."

Both Javad and my brother, whom I was talking to regularly, were against my returning.

"They'll arrest you at the airport," Javad said. "It's mayhem here. It's too dangerous."

I wasn't really frightened of going to prison. I knew that it would be politically too costly for the state to keep a Nobel laureate imprisoned for too long and I'd be released after a spell. But the intelligence agents were far too clever for that. They would arrange, as they had done in the past, for a mob to attack my house, and I would be killed in the melee.

I sat on the bed, looking out at the sea, a pale blue-gray in the twilight, and thought of a case file I had studied all those years ago. Back in 1999, when I was representing the family of a dissident couple who had been murdered by rogue intelligence agents, I had come across the death squad's assassination list in the state's files. The couple whose family I represented had been stabbed to death in their home in November 1998; in the three weeks following their death, three dissident writers turned up dead in the outskirts of Tehran, all apparently strangled. Many felt there had to be a connection between these murders, but no one imagined it would be something as coldly systematic as a simple hit list, drawn up by state agents. Most of the writers and intellectuals who appeared on the list had already been killed, but a few names remained. Mine was one of them. The Ministry of Intelligence had formally approved my killing. The authorities had not been able to carry it out then, because the reformists began revealing the state's involvement with the death squads. But what about now, when the state was more shaken than at any moment in its history?

All these thoughts filled my head, many of them inconclusive and contradictory. On the one hand, I thought, if the Islamic Republic is praying for my death, why should I help it along? But on the other hand, I wanted to be in Iran, among my family and colleagues. I wanted to share their fate and destiny. I packed my bag as if in a trance, unsure where it would end up.

I boarded the plane hesitantly, flying to Madrid, then to Amsterdam. There I had a three-hour layover, which I spent roaming the halls of the terminal, still unsure what to do. I stood by the departure gate, staring at the word "Tehran" on the board. And I looked with envy at all those who would fly without fear of the other side. For a while I joined the line, and then, at the last moment, I pulled back. Perhaps that was the most fateful decision of my life. I often wonder what might have gone differently, had I stepped onto that flight. I might have ended up under house arrest, like the Green Movement opposition leaders. Or perhaps I could have lent my voice to the struggle, and somehow ensured that the world kept watching.

I walked out of the departures hall and called my daughter Nargess.

"Nargess *jan,* I'm coming over," I said. And then I found a train and went to my daughter.

CHAPTER 13

Alone in the World

♦

Those early days of the demonstrations kept the world transfixed, and the images and scenes of a Middle Eastern nation rising up for freedom dominated the international news. I imagined that the protests would force Supreme Leader Khamenei to back down, to admit fraud and hold new elections. Mousavi had even agreed not to run personally, simply to open a way for Ahmadinejad to step down. But as Nargess and I watched from her flat by the river, it was clear that not only was the regime unprepared to back down, but that it intended to crush the protests.

In those tense days of late June, the state sent its full armory of police officers, security agents, and paramilitaries into the streets. They beat matrons who had been protesting peacefully; they opened fire on the unarmed crowds, composed of the young and the old, the working class and the middle class. On one street a militiaman shot a young woman called Neda Agha-Soltan, whose body crumpled in the road. People in the street managed to detain the militiaman who killed her. They took his ID card off him, to keep as evidence that he worked for the state. A passerby filmed the whole incident and posted it online; the killing of Neda went viral, and her frozen face became iconic of the brutality of that time.

By this point, everyone knew that those who were injured and went to the hospital were often arrested by the police in the emergency room. And so the injured went home, waiting to be called on and treated by doctors they knew.

Throughout, the protesting people of Iran did not resort to retaliatory violence. They knew that the slightest hint of violence toward the state would lead the regime to respond furiously, going on a killing and execution spree, as it had done in the early days of the revolution when it had been challenged by people.

And so they stayed stubbornly in the streets, chanting, "We don't want an Islamic state!" and "Death to the dictator!"

As tensions mounted and the depth of the challenge posed to the regime became more evident, many Iranians began to complain that the United States was not doing enough to support the protesters. "Why doesn't Obama say something?" people asked; they felt his response had been tepid and disappointing. Some imagined that forceful words might make a difference on the ground; some seemed to think they would carry symbolic value that would have its own importance. But I thought President Obama's cautiously worded statements were precisely the right approach. What could he have done, in the end? Was he going to send ground troops to defend the protesters? Of course not. Was he going to make weekly statements condemning the supreme leader and championing the opposition? This would have been a destructive course to take. It would have emboldened the establishment figures and led them to call the opposition American stooges, and it would have risked creating a rift between the opposition leaders and the Iranian people. The president's subtle yet pointed remarks, I felt, reflected a sophisticated understanding of the internal dynamic inside Iran. In the end, those who were crushing the protesters weren't able to exploit America's response to intensify their crackdown.

I spoke regularly to the world media throughout this tumult. I kept in close touch with friends and colleagues in Tehran, and in endless interviews and appearances I relayed what was happening. Soon the authorities began regularly summoning two of my colleagues for interrogations. Through them, the government sent a message to me: "Tell Ebadi that if she stays neutral about this, we'll leave her alone. After things settle down, we'll even let her open the center back up. But the condition is that she stay silent."

I sent this message back: "I haven't supported any particular politician in this fight. What I support is the people, and their rights as citizens. Of course I cannot stay silent in the face of these ongoing killings and brutality. The center has value as a sanctuary. If I am to be silent and not defend my people, why would I need an office?"

The security officials' proposition had conveyed an important point: they didn't want me to speak up about the abuses that were going on. They found this threatening and wanted my silence. Why should I fulfill their wish? Especially since every day, more horrifying news came out of Iran.

Many of the arrested protesters were taken to a makeshift detention center called Kahrizak, which in the Iranian imagination is now a name that haunts, like Abu Ghraib. It was a large prefabricated warehouse divided into many small rooms, and the authorities packed prisoners into these spaces, often denying them access to a toilet. Torture, here, was systematic and brutal. The guards sodomized male prisoners with bottles and batons and raped the women. Several detainees died under these circumstances, including the son of a high-ranking official who happened to be an Ahmadinejad supporter. It was when this boy was killed that the political establishment started to pay attention. When the victims had been only *gheir-khodi,* outsiders with no affiliation to the state, the regime had been unmoved.

By the end of July 2009, Iranians finally retreated from the streets. As the reports emerged of the rapes and abuse at Kahrizak, people came to understand exactly the price they would pay for challenging the regime. The majority decided that they were not willing to give their lives or have them broken, but their grievances festered. Each evening across the city, people started taking to the rooftops of their buildings and crying *"Allaho akbar"* into the night. To shout "God is great" from your rooftop in an Islamic country should not, the thinking went, be a punishable offense; but in this collective action, in hearing the echoes reverberate across the streets and throughout neighborhoods, people signaled to one another, and to the state, that they had not forgotten. The slogan "Death to the dictator" was etched in their hearts.

Ahmadinejad, intoxicated with his victory, called his opponents *khas o khashak,* nothing but "dust and dirt." In the short term, he could easily claim success; as president, he'd crushed the widest and most significant popular uprising Iran had witnessed since the Islamic Revolution. Khamenei declared his unstinting support for Ahmadinejad, and the Revolutionary Guards, who had handled the repression and bolstered the system, acquired even more power than before. The president appointed a number of guardsmen to cabinet positions, and the Revolutionary Guards' economic clout, already considerable, expanded even further. But the moral victory belonged to the protesters, and mainstream public sentiment shifted palpably from indifference toward the regime to real revulsion. The foremost classical musician of Iran, Mohammad Reza Shajarian, sided openly with the "dust and dirt" and asked state television to stop airing his music; a musician of the younger generation wrote a song called "Khas o Khashak" that quickly went viral.

By that point, I was speaking to Javad every night on the phone. I either called when I knew he would be home from work or he called Nargess's flat himself. One night he told me that a court summons had arrived for me.

"I told them that you're not even in the country," he said.

"It's just another warning. They want me to be quiet."

Between the interrogation and later detention of my colleagues and the scale and severity of the torture at Kahrizak, I knew I could not return to Iran anytime soon. And this saddened me immensely. How was I going to be able to give up my Tehran? After all, I was someone who had stayed put in Iran even under the most difficult conditions. Even during the Iran-Iraq War and during the days when Tehran was under a barrage of missiles, I didn't leave my country. I was the one who had always been opposed when my friends chose to emigrate. I hadn't left Iran with the intention of staying away. I had left with only carry-on luggage.

The sadness did not get better with the passage of time. Each day, I stared out at the colors of the houses, neat rows of cinnamon and tulip red, and felt a tremendous dislocation. Nargess had decorated her small flat, which, in the Dutch style, had a sink in the main room, with Iranian kilims and tiles, but despite being surrounded by all these textiles and colors of home, I felt terribly dislocated.

One morning, I looked in the bathroom mirror and noticed that the right side of my throat, just under my jaw, was swollen. A large, walnut-sized lump jutted out. It wasn't painful, but of course the first thing that comes to one's mind is cancer, especially since I had lost my sister to cancer. I needed to see a doctor. But who? I had no medical insurance in the Netherlands.

Several days later, I mentioned my problem to a friend, who introduced me to a specialist in The Hague, a physician who knew and respected my work. He received me graciously and refused to accept a fee. After some examination and an MRI, he concluded that nervous tension was causing my saliva ducts to become blocked. He prescribed a tranquilizer, which was moderately useful. But it did not address the key problem. My great sorrow arose from being so far from Iran, and no medicine could alleviate this pain.

Some days, when the sun was setting, I imagined I heard the sound of the call to prayer, the *azaan,* as we say in Persian. I thought perhaps there was a local mosque, and I would search for it. But I soon realized there was none nearby; it had only been my mind producing the sounds of the familiar. Sometimes I would overhear people speaking in a shop and would think that I'd picked up a scrap of Persian; but when I listened again, I was usually wrong. So I did the only thing I knew how to: I worked harder. I went on more trips, delivered more speeches, gave more interviews. With work I could just manage, most of the time, to keep the darkness at bay.

CHAPTER 14

Betrayal

♦

In August 2009, Nargess and I left The Hague to spend a month with Negar, who was still living in Atlanta. Nargess had been accepted into a PhD program in London that would start in September, and she wanted to spend some time with her sister before the move to Britain. We arrived in the high heat of summer, and spent most of our days in Negar's cool, air-conditioned apartment. Her place had floor-to-ceiling windows that overlooked a lush green park. This was where I liked to sit when talking on the phone; I would watch the children kick balls about or ride their bikes while holding popsicles.

The telephone had become for me, as perhaps it does for most exiles, the lifeline through which I connected with almost every part of me that mattered. I usually spoke to Javad two or three times a week, on

appointed days. He had a special separate SIM card exclusively for my calls, bought under someone else's
name, to make it difficult for the authorities to trace.
We avoided landlines, which I had come to think of as
simply speakers plugged into the Ministry of Intelligence listening room.

One Monday I wasn't able to reach him during our
usual time, but I wasn't unduly concerned. He often
went on short trips for the consulting work he did or
spent long weekends at our orchard cottage with
friends. The mobile reception there was weak, and we
generally didn't talk until he was back in Tehran. During the course of that week, however, I still did not
manage to speak to him. I called my sister in Tehran,
Nooshin, and asked her to check on our apartment,
but she found no sign of him. He didn't answer either
of his mobile phones; I even tried our home landline,
but it just rang and rang.

Then Nooshin called me to say that she had knocked
and found him at home. She said he had just returned
from a trip, was unwell, and was going straight
to bed.

The next day, Javad reached me on my mobile while
I was in Negar's apartment.

"Shirin?" His voice was tense and shaky.

"Where have you been? Nooshin has been looking
for you!"

"Shirin, I don't know if you can forgive me. Or
maybe we've reached the end of the line." I could hear
him breathing shallowly.

"Are you crying?" My fingers unconsciously flew up to my throat, where the walnut bulge had finally subsided. "What's happened?"

"Will you forgive me?"

"Javad, tell me first what's happened!"

He began to explain, in a crushed, flattened voice, what had transpired in the nearly two weeks since we had last spoken. This is what my husband of thirty-four years relayed to me:

He had been feeling, in his words, "very lonely and empty." One evening a friend of his, a Ms. Jeyhani, had noticed that he was not doing terribly well and had invited him over to her apartment.

"Very unexpectedly, a mutual friend, Nazi, also stopped by." Javad's voice dropped off, and he paused for a moment before continuing.

"Between Nazi and me . . . a romantic relationship used to exist. But I had not seen her for a very long time. Years. We had stopped our relationship. But Ms. Jeyhani thought we should get back together. She kept pouring us more to drink and saying that we were both going through difficult times and could support each other. She kept stressing that now that my wife was gone, I was all alone and needed someone to show me some affection."

Apparently, at that point, this Ms. Jeyhani said she had an appointment and left her flat, suggesting that Javad and Nazi stay until she got back.

"We realized she'd left us alone on purpose. Nazi

started taking her clothes off, hugging me, saying how much she had missed me."

Javad paused, but I said nothing.

"Shirin, are you there? Are you listening?"

I had gone completely silent. I had never suspected Javad of having cheated on me. By nature I was never a suspicious wife, and I'd never permitted myself to scan his email in-box or his address book. He had never raised questions about my male colleagues, and I'd accorded him the same understanding. It had seemed to work for us, this mutual respect. Until now. I kept staring at the coffee table, with its magazines and a Rembrandt coaster and lavender pastilles; all of it looked exactly the same as it had five minutes ago. How could it look the same?

"Go on."

"She kept touching me . . . and I . . . I succumbed to the situation. We were embracing in the bedroom when suddenly the door of the second bedroom of the apartment burst open. Mahmudi, the intelligence agent, and two cameramen came in. I rushed to stand up, but they said that everything—our entire conversation, the whole event—had been recorded on film. I was so scared, Shirin, I thought I was going to collapse."

I leaned my head into my hands and closed my eyes. I thought of Mahmudi standing over my husband in that apartment, gloating, finally victorious. The image enraged me. I was far, far angrier with Mahmudi and his agents than I was with Javad.

Javad was now crying openly, stopping every few seconds to draw a breath before continuing.

"I didn't know what to do. Mahmudi called someone; he told some officers who were apparently waiting downstairs in the street to come up. He told Nazi and me to get dressed. I fumbled and got my clothes on. In a couple of minutes the apartment was full of agents. They handcuffed me and tied a blindfold around my eyes. I stumbled downstairs with them, and they pushed me into a car. They forced my head down, so that no one would see me."

"What happened to . . . that woman? And your host?" I tried to keep the rage out of my voice, but I couldn't bring myself to say her name.

"They only arrested me. I'm sure Jeyhani was cooperating with them. How else could they have set up all their equipment before I even got there? I can't really be sure about Nazi. All I know is they didn't arrest her."

Javad described how they took him straight to Evin Prison, where I had visited so many clients over the years and where I had been detained for twenty-five days. He said they made him strip down and lie flat on a wooden bench. And then they lashed his bare back for drinking alcohol that evening. Did the lasher hold a Koran under his arm, to prevent him from using too much force? I forgot to ask this. Or perhaps Javad was still blindfolded and did not see.

And then they led him to a cell, with nothing to treat the bloody welts on his back, and left him in a solitary confinement cell, perhaps only slightly bigger than the size of an ordinary bathtub. It was so small he could traverse the length in two strides, the carpet dirty and yellowed and smelling of dampness. It had no mattress, but they gave him one blanket. This is a little bit of meanness that I recalled from my own time in solitary confinement at Evin, because the one blanket means you have the choice of either rolling it up as a pillow, and then sleeping in the cold, or using it to cover yourself, and developing neck and back pain from the lack of head support. Either way, the arrangement is meant to inflict sleeplessness and discomfort.

For two full days, Javad was left alone in his cell. He ran his fingers over the cement walls and looked expectantly at the small window that permitted the guards to look in, but no one came. The fluorescent lights in his cell and in the corridor were on around the clock, so he started losing his sense of night and day. He began to grow paranoid. The bread and tea they brought for breakfast, he suspected, was intended to throw him off; that meal meant it was probably really evening.

On the third day, two prison guards came to his cell. They blindfolded him and pushed a stick into his hands; he held on to one end and a guard held the other, as they walked down the corridor, twisting and turning, up stairs and down. Finally they arrived at a room where they took his blindfold off, a sort of courtroom without windows. A bearded cleric, the judge, sat behind a wooden desk, and next to him a court clerk.

The judge, in his early fifties, with an angular chin and a patchy beard, looked narrowly at Javad. "I've watched the entire film. There's really no room for denial. You are a married man and have committed adultery. According to Article 225 of the Islamic Penal Code, you are sentenced to death by stoning. The sentence will be carried out two days from now."

"I want a lawyer," Javad said. "I'm not going to do anything without a lawyer."

"A lawyer!" the judge said, amused. "What for? What is a lawyer going to say? We have a film of you, sir—your entire liaison is on camera! What kind of defense do you imagine you could mount? Just go. Go be ashamed of yourself, and spend your last two days repenting to God. At least your spirit won't be wretched and tormented after you die."

The whole trial took about twenty minutes. Iranian judges scarcely ever handed down stoning verdicts, but the situation seemed to require an especially horrific punishment. Afterward, they blindfolded Javad again and led him back to his cell with the stick. As he recounted the terror of being back in the cell, the numbness of not knowing when it was day and when it was night, the suffocating sense of quiet, the cement walls, the lack of anything to read or even look at, I felt a stab of grief. Those who have served time call solitary confinement "white torture," and ordinary people like Javad suffer the most, because they have not prepared themselves. The political and civic activists we trained at the center knew to expect this. They readied themselves beforehand, practicing mental tricks and ways of coping; they knew what to do to ward off the panic. Javad had had none of that. He had never been particularly interested in politics and had never involved himself in my cases; he worked hard, and when he had time left over, he filled it with music and culture.

The day, or some lengthy time that felt like a day, after the trial, Mahmudi, the man who had devoted his life to destroying mine, came to Javad's cell. He was accompanied by his boss, a man who introduced himself by the pseudonym of Farahani.

When Mahmudi saw Javad crumpled against the side of the cell, unshaven, his hair greasy, with dark circles under his eyes, his eyes lit up.

"Now Ebadi can see the result of her activities," he said grandly, as though announcing a personal victory to a crowd. "I warned her so many times. So many times I told her, 'You need to shut up.' But she never listened."

Javad pulled himself up, so as not to speak to them from the floor.

"Why should I be responsible for what my wife does? What kind of dirty games are you trying to play with me? Because of my wife, you harass me like this, in the name of Islam?"

Mahmudi's eyes darkened. He lunged toward Javad, punching him in the face. He slapped his head, punched his face again.

"Don't you dare ever mention Islam again, do you hear me?" He shoved him back against the cell wall and kicked him in the stomach.

"The word 'Islam' is dirty in your mouth. For God's sake, how can you even say it? You, who've violated sharia in the most disgusting way. . . . You haven't even prayed once since you've been here! You dare question our Islam?"

They had been filming him in his cell, Javad realized. How else would they know he hadn't prayed, not even a single time? He brushed a hand against his mouth to wipe away the blood oozing out of his gashed lip, then raised his arms to protect his head.

"I swear on the Koran, I don't know anything about what Shirin is up to. Don't punish me for what she does."

Mahmudi was panting, tired from the blows. "Ebadi used to say that she had no dark spot. She was so proud of that, thought she was invincible. Now she'll see what a big weakness she has."

When Javad saw that pleading or protesting would only provoke Mahmudi to beat him more, he asked what it was they wanted from him.

For the first time, Farahani spoke. He was a wide man, with a considerable gut, a gleaming forehead, and eyebrows that formed a continuous line.

"You're starting to see what the problem is. If you're still defending your wife, it means you're her ally and collaborator. And you should be punished as such. If the truth is otherwise, you need to prove that to us. We need to hear that you think differently than she does."

"You need to hear about that?" It sounded too easy to Javad.

"Well, we need some good evidence of that. You need to go in front of the camera and say the things that I ask you to say. If you do as I say, we'll let you go."

"But what about the court's verdict?"

Farahani barked a laugh. "My word has more authority around here than the court verdict. You just do the interview, learn your lines, and you can go free as soon as we're done."

He took a piece of paper from a manila folder he was carrying and handed it to Javad.

"Memorize this. Say it enough times that you can say it on camera tomorrow morning from memory."

"Rest up," Mahmudi said as they left the cell, clanging the metal door hard behind himself.

Javad sank down to the floor, folding the blanket beneath himself. The piece of paper contained this statement:

Shirin Ebadi did not deserve to receive the Nobel Prize. She was awarded the prize so that she could help topple the Islamic Republic. She is a supporter of the West, particularly America. Her work is not in the service of Iranians, but serves the interests of foreign imperialists who seek to weaken Iran.

His fingers, still bloody from the gash on his mouth, left reddish-brown prints on the white page. The paragraph read straight out of an Islamic Republic playbook—the language was the stuff of the *Kayhan* newspaper or state TV, the regime's two main propaganda outlets. He would recite it as instructed, he thought, but everyone would surely know that he had been pressured into saying those things. They would understand that the person he had been all his life until that moment had not suddenly ceased to exist but was just parroting something he had been forced to memorize.

He slept fitfully that night, the cold of the floor seeping into his bones. At some hour before dawn, a prison guard arrived, and Javad's transformation began. He was given the clothes he had arrived in at the prison, and permitted a shower. A barber shaved his beard and tidied his hair. A guard blindfolded him and led him through to another room, Javad again negotiating a maze of corridors with the aid of a stick. Here, when they lifted the cloth off his eyes, he saw what looked like a television set: a staged living room, comfortable armchairs, a side table with a vase of plastic pink roses. Directly opposite the armchairs was a video camera.

Mahmudi was waiting, sitting in one of the armchairs, his arms spread on the armrests in a sultan's pose.

"Nothing to worry about. You've seen a camera before, right? It's that easy."

Javad felt queasy, but he sat in front of the camera and, when instructed, started reciting his paragraph.

"No, no, no," the cameraman cut in. "That's too wooden. It's no use to us if you read it like that! Try again, more naturally."

Javad began again, trying to inject some cadence into his voice: "Shirin Ebadi did not deserve to win the Nobel—"

Mahmudi got up and smacked the flat of his hand across the back of Javad's head.

"You're so stupid you can't even recite a simple text? Come on. We don't want to be here all day."

After six more takes, Mahmudi considered Javad's performance acceptable. Once again, Javad was blindfolded, handed the stick, and led back to his cell. This worried him. They had promised that he would be released immediately after the filming. A few minutes later, Mahmudi's boss came to his cell.

"Now that you've become a good boy, listen carefully to the plan," Farahani said. "Tomorrow morning after breakfast, you'll go to your house with one of our staff to pick up your passport, birth certificate, and every document or ownership deed that you have in your name or your family's name. You bring them here, and after that you'll be freed. The court verdict is also easy. You and Nazi go to an address that I will give you; there, a cleric will issue a certificate of temporary marriage backdated by five years. You'll bring that certificate here, ask for it to be included in your file, and tell the judge that the lady in question was married to you on a temporary basis. That'll take care of the unlawful sexual liaison. At the most, you will be fined one hundred thousand *tomans* for not registering your temporary marriage certificate."

They then released him to go home, and by six o'clock he was back in our Tehran living room.

As he drew to the end of the story, his breath was coming in bursts, and he was speaking with lots of pauses and breaks. He sounded wrecked, nothing like the confident, athletic, playful husband of the many years of our marriage.

He was waiting for me to say something, but I was, for perhaps the first time in my life, unable to come up with a single thing. As a woman, a wife, I was sick with anger. He had betrayed me. But I was even more furious, more floored, by the depth of evil of the intelligence agents. Their malice and cunning truly had no limit; they were prepared to do anything—crush people's children, their marriage—to achieve their ends. Tears slid down my face, but I tried not to make any noise.

What did they want from me? I didn't permit myself that thought very often. But it came careening into my head, and I wanted to run out onto the balcony and scream it. How much could they take away from one person? They had taken my judgeship, my entire life's ambition; when I resurrected myself and built a human rights center, they took that, too; with their violence and electoral fraud, I had lost my homeland. And now they had tried to take away my husband. I closed my eyes, wanting nothing but to go to sleep. I longed to put my head on a pillow and let the tiredness wash over me, so that just for a little while I wouldn't have to think about it. But Javad was talking again, asking me—me!—for advice about his pending stoning sentence.

"What do you think I should do?"

"I don't see any option but to do as they've asked," I said. "But, of course, only if . . . that woman . . . agrees."

Javad said he would try to contact her and would let me know what happened.

"I'll be waiting to hear from you," I said.

"I'll call soon."

I waited to hear back. Moving around the apartment, I thanked God for small graces. That Nargess had not been home when Javad called, and that she would—at least for a time—be spared knowing what had been done to her parents. Negar and her husband left the house early and didn't return until evening, so their ears were safe.

I sat on the sofa looking out across the park, mechanically checking news websites every hour. I felt as though I were in some sort of daze, bewildered and swinging between rage and a low-lying guilt. Even this I interrogated. Was I right to feel guilty? The intelligence apparatus had simply pushed themselves to the furthest reaches of their inhumanity, but was it not

Javad who had fundamentally betrayed me? But I was not in his shoes, isolated, away from my wife and daughters, vulnerable. I thought of telling him that he was not alone—that we were not alone. That I knew of many cases where the intelligence ministry had done the same sorts of things to others, used sexual black-mail and traps of all sorts, in order to force dissident politicians out of public life or simply to wound and silence critics. But knowing this didn't lessen my anger, and I doubted that it would lessen his pain. I had no answers, just a dull ringing ache in my neck.

That night, when Nargess came home, I said nothing. I knew she would eventually need to know, but I was in shock and could not yet form the words to tell her. Sparing her, even for a few days, was all I could do. I held on, despite the breathlessness that seized me in the mornings when I woke up and remembered.

A week later, Javad called again and told me how things had gone. He had telephoned Nazi—he said her name, I did not—and she had agreed to go with him to see the cleric specified by the intelligence agents. The cleric, as promised, issued a backdated temporary mar-riage certificate that showed them, at the date of film-ing, to have been *sigheh,* or temporarily married. Iranian law allows for two types of marriage, conven-tional and temporary. Under *sigheh,* the duration of the marriage is determined in advance; it could be as short as an hour or as long as a decade. If a child is born under a *sigheh* marriage, he or she is a rightful child, with all legal entitlements from both parents. When the *sigheh* expires, the "married couple" should separate, unless the arrangement is mutually extended. The practice has existed in Iran for centuries and is primarily intended to determine and regulate paternity, should a woman become pregnant. But it is shunned by younger and less traditional Iranians, who see it as an archaic religious loophole that effectively legalizes prostitution.

Javad had taken the certificate back to the court at Evin, which, in turn, fined him 100,000 *tomans,* precisely the amount Mahmudi's boss had specified. So now the punishment they had dangled over him, execution by stoning, the punishment they had used to force him to denounce me before the cameras, was null. But he had been required to turn over his passport and was barred from leaving the country.

In the days that followed, we talked several times. But I felt as though I were speaking to a stranger. Javad was broken, pleading during each conversation for me not to leave him. He sounded so unwell that regardless of my own feelings, which were still too raw and fresh for me to even contemplate a decision, I was worried for him. Mahmudi had not yet released the denunciation, and the threat of it dangled over our heads. I encouraged him to get out of Tehran, to spend some time with friends, to finally go visit the desert areas of Iran he had always wanted to explore. He did travel a bit, though each time he came back, he said the same thing:

"I miss you and the girls, I want to see you. But Mahmudi has my passport. I have to convince him to give it back, so I can come see you all."

How he would manage that, I did not know.

In those first couple of weeks after Javad told me what had happened, we spoke on the phone regularly, and often on Skype. Nargess had been out during the very first phone call, but most of the others she overheard. She wanted to know what was going on. I had no choice but to explain, and one morning after Negar left for work, I sat Nargess down on the couch. I avoided going into any detail, and I tried to tell her in a way that would not be overly distressing. She had her own worries, and I didn't want to add to them.

"Why don't you tell Negar?" she said.

"Well, because your sister is busy with her PhD. And she can't do anything about the situation anyway, so I think we shouldn't worry her."

"I think she should know."

"Let's see what happens, and whether they end up broadcasting your dad's confession. Remember, Negar has a new husband—she might feel embarrassed in front of him and her new in-laws." I worried about this in particular: the possibility my daughters would be embarrassed or feel awkward because of what had transpired between their parents.

"I wish you'd tell her. So I could have someone to talk with about it."

She unwound her long black hair, pulled at its ends, and then gathered it up again.

"Why would he do such a thing and speak against you? Why would he go with that woman?" She kept repeating these questions, growing more agitated.

I decided to be as frank with her as I knew how to be. Her work in The Hague involved her researching and documenting terrible atrocities. She helped prepare files and witnesses' statements involving descriptions of extreme violence. I felt that she needed to see how that work, the work she wanted to make her future, connected to what she was experiencing in her family. The field of human rights is not about pretty words; it involves the abuse of the vulnerable by those who wield power. That was the fine line that connected massacres in Sarajevo to atrocities in Sierra Leone to the systematic persecution of dissidents in places like Iran and Russia.

I told her that if she wanted to be a human rights lawyer and activist, she had to cultivate the culture of that world inside herself. She had to understand what that world involved, in all its depth and occasional blackness.

"Human beings are free, Nargess. But each individual has only a certain threshold for suffering. Your father couldn't take that kind of torture."

She crossed her arms over her chest tightly, and listened.

"This could have happened to any man," I said. "This is something between him and me. But you have to look at it differently. You should be wondering why an intelligence agent was hiding with a camera in the second bedroom. Were the country's problems resolved by determining who was cheating on whom? This was a trap they used against me, and that is how you must think about it."

It was a bitter lesson to impart to my own daughter. But she wanted to become an activist herself, to use her knowledge of the law to defend Iranians. She had to know exactly what she, and all the other young women and men taking up such a struggle, would be up against.

CHAPTER 15

Life Without a Home

♦

In September 2009, Nargess began her PhD in London at the School of Oriental and African Studies. She found a small flat near the Thames, and I eventually followed her there to make London a base for my travels. Around the same time, Negar and her husband moved from Atlanta to Boston to take a research position at MIT. I traveled most of the year, but when I wasn't on the road, I divided my time between their two cities. Negar complained a bit that I spent more time in Europe, but this was simply because Europe dealt with Iran more closely and there were more arenas in which to pursue human rights advocacy.

Often I ended up in Geneva, where a number of United Nations bodies that I dealt with were based. One bright morning in late September, I dressed and went out into the street, wanting to be around people, to feel the bustle of a city, even if it was not my own. I walked toward the water, watching the early sunlight glint off the wheels of the bicycles and the boats anchored in the lake list gently. I sat in a café and ordered an espresso, a short, bitter European preparation that I had grown to like. The habit provided a jolt that carried me into the day. A woman went past holding the hands of two children, weighed down with schoolbags, hurrying them along as they dawdled to point at two birds bobbing their heads along a window ledge. In Persian we have an expression: "to sit at the foot of your life and home." Broadly, it means that your life is your home life. I realized that if I didn't have a home life, I still had my other life, my work, and I needed to get back to it.

I rested my head on my hands for a moment, to collect myself. I found it hard to get the flashing faces out of my mind. The face of Neda Agha-Soltan, who had been shot down in the street during the protests following the election. Javad's face. The smile my colleague Narges Mohammadi always flashed when she entered the office. She had been arrested on the very first day of the protests.

I must have looked utterly bereft, because the young woman at the table next to me leaned over.

"Are you all right?" she asked uncertainly, in English.

My English was more halting at the time, but I tried to respond: "I don't know if you follow the news. I come from Iran, and there have been bitter events in my country."

She smiled and reached out to touch my arm gently. "I understand. I'm Palestinian. I know what it's like to have constant sorrow for your homeland."

We sat together talking. She was living in France with her family and had come to Geneva for work. I told her a bit about Iran and what the country was going through; she spoke about Palestine and her relatives scattered across the world. And something in that conversation, a connection to a stranger who I would never have guessed might have related so intimately to some part of my own story, buoyed me.

Two days later, I was meeting with the U.N. high commissioner for human rights, Navi Pillay. We had met several times before, and she was eager to know about the latest developments in Iran. I gave her details about the numbers of arrests, the conditions of the detention centers, the harassment of activists, and the persecution of ordinary Iranians whose only crime had been to show up at a few demonstrations. I told her about the militia gangs who roamed neighborhoods, smashing the cars of those who dared shout *"Allaho akbar"* from their rooftops in the evenings. She asked me to explain some Iranian laws to her, so she could understand how these abuses fit into the legal context of the Islamic Republic itself. I was pleased that she was so thorough, and I spent much of that day with one of her deputies, an Iranian by background, going through the laws and contraventions one by one.

As I left the building, I saw that a group of Iranians were staging a protest rally outside. In the months that followed the events of June 2009, Iranians across much of the world, from Los Angeles to Prague, held such demonstrations in solidarity with the Green Movement protesters inside Iran. One of the organizers saw me and ran over, asking if I would address the crowd. There were perhaps a hundred people, and many of them simply held aloft photographs of people killed in the recent events, like Sohrab Aarabi, with his glasses and green scarf, who had been shot in the chest on June 15.

I took the loudspeaker, and the minute I started to say something, all I could see was the sea of images in front of me, the faces of all these innocent young people who had lost their lives. It was a reflection of the carousel of images that usually just ran through my head. I thought of the courage it had taken for those young people in Tehran to go out into the streets holding those simple placards—"Where is my vote?"—with the openness and simplicity of a child, only to be razed down by bullets. Iranians had shown themselves to be peaceful in their resistance, I told the crowd, and their determination would one day bring about change. Of this, I was certain. It was the first time in my life I had cried while speaking before a crowd. Unfortunately, it was not the last.

It was after that trip to Geneva that my unending trips started, and they continue to this day. I live in airports, one day at the European Parliament, the next at the European Commission; after that, various universities in South America, other sites across the globe.

When I left Geneva, it felt good to be working so much again. In Tehran I often worked fourteen-hour days, because I had tangible cases to take forward. With each of these trips, it began to feel as though my work in exile still had a concrete purpose. Wherever I went I told my audience about what was happening in Iran, and how state censorship meant that the world heard little, or not enough, about what Iranians were going through. I was gradually joined in exile by thousands of Iranians who'd had to flee in the wake of those 2009 protests. Journalists, activists, lawyers, doctors, even dentists, students, and ordinary people whose lives had been cast into disarray, for often vague, barely political connections to the events of those months.

Often these people sought me out, asking how I had managed. I told them that, like me, they needed to focus on work and avoid dwelling on the grief of their dislocation. I saw us as similar to people who'd boarded a ship that sank, leaving everyone swimming in deep waters. We had no choice but to swim; to become tired simply was not an option, as that meant drowning. I told them not to think about the shore and how far it was, how it wasn't even visible, because this would just bring on despair.

That is our situation. Swimming in the darkness,

not giving in to the pessimism and thoughts of the far-off shore.

Javad followed the clerk at Tejarat Bank to the vault of our safe-deposit box, passing the staff members typing away at their desks. As they approached the vault, with its heavy steel door, the bank manager ran over to them, a troubled look on his face.

"I'm afraid we won't be able to allow you access today," he said.

"To our box? Why ever not?" Javad was taken aback. He had gone to put in some documents.

"A letter has come from the judiciary ordering us to deny access. I'm very sorry."

"How do I know our belongings are safe?"

"I can't say anything more."

Javad went back to his car and called me. "They've confiscated your Nobel medal," he said.

I was flabbergasted, for it was almost impossible to contemplate what they imagined they would gain from such a crude move. The world press began covering the story around the clock, and newspapers ran caricatures of Ahmadinejad embracing my medal, saying, "I finally got my wish, and a medal too!" "This is the first time a Nobel Peace Prize has been confiscated by national authorities," the Norwegian foreign minister said, calling the state's move shocking.

The furor swelled to such a pitch and became such a global embarrassment to the regime that about ten days later, Mahmudi called Javad and told him to come to the bank.

"Enough of this—we'll open up the damn box," the interrogator told him.

Mahmudi was waiting for Javad at the bank, together with a camera crew. They stood by the vault while the poor bank manager, a kind man who knew us well and seemed to find all of this excruciating, examined a letter from the court allowing access to the box. Two keys were required to open the box, as usual, and with the cameras rolling, Javad and the manager both inserted their keys.

"Where's the medal? Show us the medal," Mahmudi demanded.

Javad, now being paraded before the state's cameras for the second time, took the medal out of the box and handed it to Mahmudi, who held it up before the camera. He then handed it back to Javad.

"Put it back," he told him. Javad put it back in the box, and the cameraman recorded the medal's return and turned off his camera.

"Now lock it up," Mahmudi ordered the bank manager.

"Wait, you said the box was to be opened! I need some documents, and I have some things to put in."

The box contained virtually everything of importance that we had accumulated during our thirty-four-year marriage. It had deeds and documents, the gold coins my daughter Negar had received at her wedding, some family jewelry.

"We unlocked the safe-deposit box and returned the Nobel medal," Mahmudi said, laughing. "Now we have it on film and will send it to any international figure who opens his mouth to object. So your wife can stop spreading lies about this government, pretending we've taken away her prize."

Javad was furious. "This safe-deposit box is in my name. Mine. And it holds my assets, which haven't been confiscated. How do my family documents, or my marriage certificate, have anything to do with state security?"

"I'm the one who makes that call."

Mahmudi and his crew turned and walked out, taking the second key with them. Javad felt faint; his blood pressure had dropped. The bank manager led him to his office, where he offered Javad some sugar water.

As they sat in the office together, the bank manager chided him.

"Why are you still here? Don't you see there's no law, just bullying everywhere? You should leave. Forget everything in the safe. Just go!"

"It's not actually my choice. My passport has been confiscated, and I'm banned from leaving. I'm stuck because I married a woman who believes in human rights and isn't prepared to back down. And in the eyes of those intelligence agents, there's no greater sin. There's nothing for me to do. Neither she nor they are willing to compromise."

When Javad recounted all of this to me, he sounded truly tired and fed up. His daily life now consisted of doing small renovations on our apartment and at the orchard house, hiking and swimming with friends, and having dinner with his sisters. We never spoke of my returning to Tehran, as even despite the Nobel Prize, it was almost certain I would be immediately arrested. But not discussing any prospect of return also felt like a passive acknowledgment that we would probably never be together again.

For Javad, the hounding and the harassment were just building, it seemed, after his terrible ordeal, instead of letting up. He had even tried to take some steps himself, going to see a relative who had formerly been deputy speaker of the parliament, to lodge a complaint against Mahmudi and all he had done. But nothing this relative did had any traction at all. In the Islamic Republic, everything could be forgiven in the name of safeguarding "security." Of course, "security" had now become a hollow word, just a euphemism for the system's absolute political power and its crushing of all criticism.

At eleven-thirty on a cold night that December, just a few days after Christmas, Mahmudi and his agents rapped at the door of my sister Nooshin's house in Tehran. She and her husband had just brushed their teeth and were getting ready for bed.

"We've come to ask Khanoum Ebadi a few questions," one of them said.

"Do you have a warrant?" her husband asked. The late hour made him even more nervous.

They presented a sheet of paper signed by the Tehran chief prosecutor, authorizing them to interrogate whomever they needed to, to search wherever was necessary, and to make arrests as appropriate.

"But the warrant doesn't mention anyone's name," Nooshin said, alarmed.

"Exactly—that means we can arrest anyone, including you," Mahmudi said, grinning.

His men started going through the house, pulling open the cutlery drawer in the kitchen, rifling through the pantry. The laptops they found went straight into their duffel bags. And then Mahmudi told Nooshin that she needed to come with him to the "ministry" for interrogation.

"It'll only take a couple hours," he said. "You can come home after. We'll just go through the laptops while we're talking, and if we need you again, we'll summon you."

My sister Nooshin is a dentist with two sons. Between her practice, some research work, and taking care of her family, she really doesn't have time to be doing anything politically subversive. And that night, as the clock edged past midnight, she was scared to go with those men. What legitimate government building would be open at that hour? But in the end, she went, because she knew that resisting would be useless; they would just force her anyway. She pulled on her manteau and head scarf, grabbed her handbag.

"Wait—I'm not letting you go alone," said her husband.

"You can come along, but you can't ride with us. It's illegal. You can follow in your own car," said Mahmudi.

But the moment the car carrying Nooshin set off, another car driven by Mahmudi's men blocked her husband's car. He roamed the city until nearly dawn, going from one police station to the next, rousing the on-duty clerk at the Tehran magistrate's court, but found no trace of the intelligence agents or his wife.

When I heard what had happened, my anger surged, and I charged out of the apartment in London to go for a walk. I couldn't sit still, knowing they had arrested the only sister I had left, the person I loved most dearly in the world after my husband and children; it tormented me to know that she was sitting in a cell in Evin Prison because of me. I walked for a very long time, until my feet ached and I was out of breath. He was going after me again, Mahmudi. He was going after her only to get to me, just as he had done with Javad.

They kept her for twenty-one days. I made extra *dua* every single day of her detention, whispering at the end, "Please, God, let them release my sister." Mahmudi didn't beat her, but his agents verbally abused her for hours on end during interrogation. They insulted her, they insulted me, they called me a lackey for America and berated me for my treason.

"Tell us everything you know about her," they said. "How can she afford to live abroad? Where does she get her money from? Why did she win the Nobel Prize? Who is she in contact with regularly?"

And each time, Nooshin said, "She's my sister; I'm

not her colleague. I don't know the kinds of things you want from me."

After two weeks, she started having heart palpitations and chest pains. She was permitted no visits with her husband, with her sons. It was strict solitary confinement for Nooshin, as it had been for me. The prison doctor gave her some medications, but her condition only worsened. In the end, fearing that she might die on them, creating an even greater headache, they let her go.

While she was in prison, I worked feverishly. With every report and press release and interview, I was communicating with Mahmudi: *You can't touch me. Nothing you do will affect me and what I do.*

When she was released, I called her and said, "Nooshie, if I take one step back, they'll think they've found my weak point. It'll just get worse for you. I know it's so hard, but we have to hold them back. If they see it has no effect on me, they'll eventually stop. But if they think they can use you against me, they'll do it forever."

She said she understood. I could tell from the tone of her voice that she did. When I heard myself saying such things, I recognized how stark and stubborn it sounded. But I was familiar with Mahmudi's mind, his tactics; I had come to know them inside out. When you are up against such people long enough, you come to think the way they do. After I had seen what they did to Javad, I'd finally understood them properly. They would grab anyone I loved and drag them to the edge of the most treacherous cliff. They would dangle them there, baiting me. And when I wouldn't be drawn in, they would eventually loosen their hold and let go. It is a painful calculation, but it is better to be dragged and let go than kept dangling at the edge forever. Had I budged even a bit, I have no doubt that's what they would have done with Nooshin and Javad, and perhaps other family members as well. I had seen it happen with others. The intelligence apparatus of a state like the Islamic Republic knows no gray area. You're either corruptible and scared or you're not.

"We want you to report back on every conversation you have with your sister," Mahmudi's boss told Nooshin before he released her. "Do you get it?"

"But we just talk about family—we never discuss her work. How useful is family news for you?"

"We'll see about that. We'll pay close attention and see how honest you are. Because, you know, we know everything about Shirin. Don't think that we have to listen to her phone." He laughed at that. "Tapping phones is passé; we're way beyond that. We have someone sitting right next to her to report back."

It was another message, intended to make me suspicious of everyone I worked with, to plant in my mind a tiny seed of doubt.

"You'll probably talk to her tonight," he went on. "Tell her that it's not too late—"

Nooshin cut him off angrily: "I've said it a thousand times: Shirin doesn't listen to anyone! Stop sending messages through me—it's useless."

For the next two years they kept her in limbo, not

setting a trial date but preventing her from traveling abroad and calling her back in for more questioning. Finally, after two years, her case went to trial. Mahmudi had told her that once the court was convened, she would probably get six months in prison.

The day of her trial, Nooshin walked into the court building with her lawyer, her stomach gurgling with nerves. At the entrance, she spotted one of her dental students and was gladdened to see a familiar face.

"But what are you doing here? Do you have a court case, too?" Nooshin asked, with some concern.

"God forbid I'd have a court case!" the girl laughed. "I was visiting my uncle—he's a judge at the revolutionary court. I'm heading to class now."

Nooshin's lawyer interrupted to ask what branch the girl's uncle presided over, and it turned out to be the same as the one handling Nooshin's case. They quickly briefed her about Nooshin's situation and asked her to put in a good word through her uncle.

Nooshin walked out of the court that day acquitted, exonerated from "conspiracy against national security through cooperation with Shirin Ebadi" and removed from the list of those barred from leaving the country. Despite the two-year-long machinations of one of the country's top spymasters, my sister evaded a prison term because she happened to teach dentistry and ran into one of her students in the courthouse lobby.

CHAPTER 16

The Forged Passport

♦

Colleagues in Tehran told me that Mahmudi was asking about my address in London; my nemesis wanted to know how I could afford to live in such an expensive city. How obsessed they were with money, I thought one gray afternoon in early 2010 as I boarded a bus headed toward Hyde Park. The bus rolled past the ornate stone buildings of Park Lane, the sky low and heavy with gray clouds. I believed they knew that I had no great sums of money hidden anywhere, that I did not receive sizable monthly transfers into my bank account from some shadowy foreign power. I rode the bus most of the time, like any other Londoner who had to be conscious of her spending. I knew the bus system so well that I often gave directions to confused tourists who asked for help.

My meeting that morning was at the Dorchester

Hotel, and it took me several minutes of walking around that end of Hyde Park before I found the place. It had yellow-and-white-striped awnings, and luxury cars lined the driveway, many of them with Persian Gulf license plates. A Bentley stopped near the glass doors, spilling out Arab women in full-length black *abayas* and a Filipino servant trailing behind holding shopping bags. The hotel had been suggested as a meeting place by an emissary of the French telecommunications company Eutelsat.

Eutelsat and I had been engaged in fraught discussions for some months. My involvement with the firm stemmed from my efforts to continue to pressure the Iranian government on human rights from the outside. In the aftermath of the 2009 uprising, Iranians had begun turning to satellite TV networks for their news, more so than ever before. State television and radio had carried little coverage of the nationwide protest movement, and what it did broadcast was highly partisan and distorted. Iranians' anger grew such that they began chanting against the state broadcaster on the streets during protests. Iranians had always watched networks like BBC Persian or Voice of America's Persian service, but the viewership figures for both networks had jumped, angering the Iranian regime and prompting it to scramble the networks' satellite signals more aggressively than in the past. The satellite that broadcast these two networks was Hot Bird, and virtually all of the estimated 70 percent of Iranians (by the regime's own figures) who had satellite TV at home

connected to this particular satellite, which was owned
and operated by Eutelsat.

As the Iranian authorities stepped up their scrambling efforts, not only did they knock BBC Persian and
VOA Persian off the air, but they also interfered with
the signals of neighboring networks that also broadcast on Hot Bird. These were other networks, other
channels in other languages that had nothing to do
with Iran, and the heads of those networks eventually
complained to Eutelsat about the interference with
their broadcasts. Eutelsat investigated, then sent a couple of letters requesting that Iran stop scrambling the
Hot Bird satellite—which, of course, Iran ignored. The
Iranian government, for its part, was also a paying client of Eutelsat, because a number of Iranian state networks were also broadcast on Hot Bird; thus Iran, as
a customer of Eutelsat, clearly felt well placed to ignore
its warnings.

Eutelsat ended up taking the easy way out. It took
VOA Persian and BBC Persian off Hot Bird and installed them both on a peripheral satellite. This way, it
protected the signals of its other customers and avoided
a confrontation with the Iranian government. But for
Iranians, this was a disaster, because now the state
could jam this other satellite without anyone else complaining. Imagine one of the very last closed societies
on earth (apart from North Korea and China, where
people's access to outside news and information is
heavily restricted) suddenly losing its main connection
to the world overnight. The calls started coming from

Tehran immediately. One colleague rang me at one in the morning, Tehran time.

"Why are you calling me at this hour?" I asked, surprised.

"Because I usually stay up late watching the news, and now I have nothing to watch," she said. "Instead of punishing the government, they've punished us."

It was true. By knocking the Persian news networks off Hot Bird, Eutelsat—a French company operating in the European Union, which avowed such commitment to universal human rights—was inadvertently creating the perfect state of affairs for the authoritarian government of Iran. So I pursued the path I've come to call "name and shame"; I started talking about Eutelsat's actions, and how regretful it was that nearly fifty million Iranians had lost access to objective, freer news.

The man I was meeting at the Dorchester, from Eutelsat, had apparently come to offer me an explanation. As we sat in the restaurant, which was gleaming with brass and padded with Persian carpets, and drank tea from delicate filigreed cups, it occurred to me that a company run by employees accustomed to such places might be keen to avoid losing customers. But I waited to hear him out.

Our meeting, however, was short and not especially productive. The Eutelsat representative told me that his firm had leased Hot Bird to another firm and that this firm had been the one that had complained about the interference issues. It sounded to me like an attempt to justify what was becoming an increasingly noticed and unpopular decision.

"The final responsibility rests with you," I said.

I left the meeting that day feeling frustrated. As I walked through the Dorchester's lobby, lined with palms and urns of roses and scented warm and sweet as a patisserie, I could not decide where to go next. For a moment, I hesitated at the curb. A gunned motorcycle raced up behind me, and I jumped back from the street in fright. For years, in Tehran, my ears had been primed for the sound of a motorbike; the state's favorite mode of killing critics and dissidents was sending an assassin on a bike. A shot or a plunged knife, the roar of the engine, and the target would be instantly slain, with witnesses often not even realizing what had happened. I inhaled deeply and told myself, *Shirin, you're not in Iran anymore.*

I was careful of my security in London. Nargess and I had moved into an apartment building with a concierge and multiple gates, a place where one simply could not get through without codes and some level of permission. I had never felt especially endangered otherwise, but habits stay in our bodies, as phantom memories in our muscles. Although my pulse still pounded, I smiled at the idea that part of me thought it was back in Iran.

Needing to go across town to an Iranian supermarket for some groceries, I decided to walk part of the way, to clear my head. I returned to London frequently enough that I was starting to feel at home in the city—

not properly at home, because I still traveled frequently and spent half my time in the States, but at home in terms of growing familiarity. I knew the patterns of the waning winter light, and I appreciated the friendliness of Londoners, so many of whom were themselves foreigners from some far-off place.

It occurred to me as I was walking through the park that I could go see Bernard Kouchner, the French foreign minister, who had also helped found Doctors Without Borders. I had met him several times, and he had been very friendly. He had always referred to me as a colleague—his organization had also won the Nobel Peace Prize—and I felt he might understand the gravity of the situation with Eutelsat. And, since the French government was a major shareholder in the company, he might be in a position to exert some influence.

The following week, Kouchner invited me to meet him in Paris. We sat together in the vaulted interior of the Ministry of Foreign Affairs building, and he listened patiently. "The Iranian government needs to be pressured not to scramble satellite signals," I said. "*They* should be punished, not the BBC."

Kouchner was sympathetic, and he raised the issue at the level of the European Union, which soon released a statement condemning Iran's scrambling efforts. But that was not the result I wanted. I didn't want an E.U. statement; I wanted the Islamic Republic penalized.

So I kept on. Wherever I went, meeting with various

officials, with Desmond Tutu, at the United Nations, I brought up this issue, of Iranians' right to free access to information and the astonishing case of the European firm that had effectively capitulated to the Iranian government. Eventually, public sentiment around Eutelsat's actions gained traction, and the firm reinstated BBC Persian and VOA Persian on Hot Bird, effectively plugging Iran back in.

The Islamic Republic learned a lesson. It learned that global public opinion could be mobilized and mounted to apply pressure to its behaviors on the world stage. It learned that it couldn't freely target global satellites hovering in the sky to enact its censorship. And I suppose it learned, dangerously enough for me, that I could effectively work for and demand accountability for Iranians' rights even from exile.

But, of course, the Islamic Republic, even when chastened, finds new ways to renew its purpose, cutting its citizens off from outside information. When it realized it could not hold up an iron curtain, shielding Iran from satellite signals, it installed mobile stations throughout the country's cities that did the same thing, only at the ground level. Instead of targeting the satellite waves as they bore down from the sky, these stations intercepted the waves just above Iranians' houses.

Iranians' concerns about the health impact of this interference over the city grew by the day. Newspapers published anxious pieces, and senior officials, including a vice president and the director of the Department of the Environment, spoke publicly about the medical risks of terrestrial jamming. This soon became a key issue of public debate and concern, the fact that the state was jeopardizing Iranians' health in order to censor what they could watch on television. This, too, proved that my work outside the country could still have a great impact on the government and what people inside the country were thinking and talking about.

In the months that had passed since Javad's ordeal, we had stayed in regular touch but had studiously avoided talking about our future. It seemed almost beside the point to discuss our marriage when we were physically separated, and my main concern throughout this period was to ensure that we were all as safe as possible. I knew that the Iranian authorities and Mahmudi were pressuring Javad intensely to disclose information about our life, and I worried that they would use whatever they might somehow glean against us. So while many of our conversations revolved around security, by February 2010, Javad wanted desperately to see me and the girls.

I didn't know what would become of our family, fragmented in this way, living apart by force, and I didn't know what would become of my marriage. To begin to think about this, we had to at least talk with each other face-to-face. But Javad's passport was still with Mahmudi. He went to see the authorities to ask for it back, along with our property deeds and birth certificates. They put him off for a month, and then, one afternoon, Javad called me in high spirits.

"I'm ready to book my flights," he said, sounding more like himself than he had in months.

"Did they give everything back?" I asked, suspicious.

"They still have the deeds, but at least I have my passport. I can fly as soon as we make plans."

The hard-line press, as though somehow privy to our family discussions, started running tabloid-style pieces about us. We were written about as "Shirin" and "Javad"—a debasing familiarity unheard of in Iranian newspapers. They wrote that I was refusing to allow Javad to come to Britain (as though this was in my power!) and that we were feuding. The sources for this drivel were anonymous, but the reports were attributed to Javad's family.

I ignored it all and focused on putting the dark days of the past year behind us. We planned for Javad to come to London, and then we would spend time with Negar. Javad wanted to meet with some old school friends in the States and Canada, to consult with them about finding working outside Iran.

He bought his Iran Air ticket for the following Wednesday. Even after everything, he still insisted on flying Iran Air, which he called "our" airline, by which he meant Iran's. I said nothing, but I was quietly pleased that so much of him hadn't changed, despite his ordeal—he was still quietly and proudly nationalistic, determined to fly the national carrier even when most Iranians who could afford it now traveled only on European airlines.

Two days before his flight, quite late at night in Tehran, he called me.

"I'm worried about going through passport control. What if they arrest me after I've gone through? The records will show that I've left the country, but I'll be nowhere. I'll have disappeared. Or what if they take my passport away at the airport?"

I could imagine him sitting on our plaid couch, a cup of tea growing cold beside him, the day's newspapers scattered on the table. In a marriage, there is so much physical closeness one takes for granted until it is gone: a hand rested on a shoulder, leaning over to reach for glasses on a side table. Now we had only these phone calls.

"There's one thing you can do. It won't solve everything, but you should do it."

I explained that he could go to the passport office and check whether his name was on the list of those individuals barred from leaving the country. There was a second list as well, held by the security forces at the airport, and this list snared those who made it past the first passport check. Javad wouldn't be able to find out about the second list, but he could at least check if he was on the first. Through interrogations and various channels, many politicians and civic and human rights activists had learned that they were on the second list; thus they stayed away from the airports, because to attempt to travel would lead to the confiscation of their passport and a trip to Evin Prison. Mohammad Khatami, the former president, was on that list, as was Simin Behbahani, a friend of mine and the nation's foremost poet, known as the "lioness of Iran."

"I'll try it," he said glumly.

I put the phone down and paced the small flat until Nargess came home, her arms full of groceries.

"I'm cooking for Dad," she said, pulling out a carton of strawberries and the white cheese he liked. Nargess was enthusiastic about cooking, and since moving to London, she had devoted a great deal of effort to learning how to prepare Iranian desserts and stews. Her cooking had become impressive, and she was eager to share her new skills with her father. I smiled and changed the subject, helping her put everything away.

The next morning, Javad went to the passport office. He handed his passport to a young policeman and asked for it to be checked against the foreign travel ban list. The young man disappeared, but within seconds he returned, a frown on his face.

"We don't deal with forged passports here." He tossed the passport across the counter toward Javad.

"Forged! This is my own passport. I've traveled on it many times."

"Well, if you travel on this, you're going to get arrested."

Javad stood there in shock. The policeman picked up a magnifying glass and flipped the passport open.

"See?" He hovered the lens over the main page and

showed Javad how his surname had been erased and rewritten. The same thing had been done with his British visa.

Javad leaned his head into his hands. "What am I supposed to do now?"

"Apply for a new one. But until then, don't use this one."

Javad called me that night to fill me in. He seemed bewildered by what was happening.

"Don't you see, Javad?" I said. "They tampered with your passport while you were in prison. They were probably hoping you'd travel on it without noticing; they would let you through the airport there, and then at Heathrow you'd have been arrested for traveling on a forged passport."

He didn't say anything, so I continued:

"That would have been ideal for them. They let you get arrested by the British border police. Then they haven't done anything to you themselves, but both of us look terrible when the news gets out that you were arrested in London for traveling into the U.K. on forged documents."

"I don't think you're right," Javad said. "You're being too cynical. If that was their plan, why would the policeman at the passport office have told me himself that it was forged?"

"Because that policeman isn't an intelligence agent. He had no idea what they were up to; he just looked at a passport you handed him. And Mahmudi probably didn't think you'd go to the passport office, so it didn't occur to him to keep the passport police in the loop."

"Maybe you're right. Though I don't know—it sounds so far-fetched." Javad sounded tired and hesitant, but he agreed to cancel his trip.

A few days later, he went to see Mahmudi and demanded to know why his passport had been returned to him doctored. Mahmudi put his feet up on the table and peered at Javad, not in the least chagrined.

"What, did you think we were just going to do nothing? While Ebadi travels around the world criticizing President Ahmadinejad, who has the blessing of our beloved leader? Should we just sit here idly and let it go? You got lucky this time. But who knows what'll happen next time. Tell your wife to cut it out; tell her to sit down and just be quiet. Tell her to come back to Iran, to return to her home and her normal life. Because if she keeps it up . . ."

At least that made it clear to Javad that the forgery had been Mahmudi's handiwork. So Javad applied for a new passport on the grounds that he had lost his old one. But when the new application went into the security system to be vetted—as is standard procedure in Iran—the Ministry of Intelligence sent word that because of security concerns, Javad Tavassolian was not permitted to leave the country.

This time, Javad channeled his fury through his pen. He wrote a scathing letter to the intelligence ministry, formally objecting to the ban on his travel. He asked, "Can you please explain to me what damage I, a seventy-year-old engineer who has spent my entire lifetime building my country, can pose to national security through a short trip to visit my family?"

A week later, Mahmudi summoned him. By now, the trek from our neighborhood to Mahmudi's office was becoming a regular journey for Javad. From behind his desk, Mahmudi waved the letter in the air, then read a passage aloud in a mock whining voice. Javad put his head in his hands and stared at the cracks in the faded linoleum.

"So now you complain against me? You don't seem to get it, do you, Mr. Tavassolian. I will only leave you alone once your wife becomes quiet. Do you think I'm dense? You think I don't know why you want to go abroad? You'll land and start giving interviews about why you publicly renounced your wife. She thinks she's smart, but I'm smarter."

"I would never give an interview. I just want to see my family, my wife and my daughters."

"Forget about it," Mahmudi snapped. "What I said stands. No foreign travel."

Javad rose and walked out of the room, saying goodbye only to preempt Mahmudi's rage at not being taken leave from properly. The drive home took him longer than usual; the streets were clogged with traffic, hulking cement mixers heading toward their construction projects, reminding Javad of the building projects he used to oversee, the status and respect he'd once enjoyed as a senior engineer of the teeming capital. He had lost his career too early because of me, had lost the stability of his marriage, had lost the right to see his daughters when he wanted to, or perhaps even at all.

And he knew now that the problem with Mahmudi was not going away. From that day on, Mahmudi summoned Javad twice a month for interrogation, each time posing the same questions, again and again: Where does she go? Who does she see? What did she tell you on the phone last night? We know you talked to her. And always, always: Where does she get her money?

CHAPTER 17

Dispossession

♦

As I traversed the capitals of Europe, working to ensure that Iranians inside the country had access to unbiased news, the siege against me continued in Tehran. One day, Javad told me that a letter had arrived from the state tax organization. It declared that the monetary award that had accompanied my Nobel Peace Prize ($1,200,000, received in 2004) was actually taxable, and that I was therefore now years in arrears and also owed years' worth of late penalties. I sighed deeply when Javad read me the letter, because I saw the direction in which this was headed. I had settled my taxes each year, and I had received my annual license to practice law on that basis. Iranian law exempts income from awards and prizes from taxation, so there was no basis to tax the Nobel money.

A friend and colleague of mine at the Defenders of

Human Rights Center, Nasrin Sotoudeh, took up the case on my behalf and went to file an objection. One visit to the tax office was enough to make clear who had concocted the charges; the tax officials told her that the *herasat,* or safeguarding, section was very sensitive about the case. *Herasat* is the term for the section of each ministry or organization across the government through which the Ministry of Intelligence exercises its influence. In other words, this case had been put together against me through orders from the intelligence ministry.

A few days after Nasrin's meeting with the tax officials, Mahmudi turned up at her office. "I don't want you defending Ebadi on this," he said.

"Prizes aren't taxable—that's just a fact," she said.

They sparred, and she refused to back down, promising to take the case to the Board of Settlement of Tax Disputes. Nasrin discovered a litany of problems and discrepancies in the case against me. They had backdated a tax warning to 2004 but had sloppily included the address from my building that had come into existence only after 2008, when the street had been renumbered.

When the case reached the Board of Settlement of Tax Disputes, the tax officials argued that the Nobel Prize is a "political" award and, as such, is taxable. Nasrin put up a detailed defense; she had also secured a letter from the Norwegian Nobel committee that confirmed that the prize is a social and scientific one, made for contributions to human rights. That should have settled the matter, but the board had decided—or been instructed in advance—that I was guilty.

Five months later, Nasrin went to prison. For agreeing to defend me, and for her other human rights work, she was sentenced to six years in prison. Though I tried to raise her case with the media and mention her during my talks and meetings, her arrest attracted only modest attention in the West. I wished that the international media paid more attention to how Iranians in the younger generation were being systematically bullied by the state into abandoning their work. The climate in which I had built up my practice and established myself no longer existed, and by meting out such a harsh sentence to Nasrin, the state was trying to intimidate the few remaining human rights lawyers who had not already gone abroad.

The court also barred Nasrin from practicing law or leaving the country for twenty years and found her guilty of "acting against national security" and of "propaganda against the regime." Apart from her recent work defending my seized assets, the main focus of Nasrin's work had been to defend Iran's most vulnerable citizens, prisoners of conscience and minors facing the death penalty.

I had known Nasrin for almost twenty years, since before she had even finished her law degree. We worked closely together for years, but my most vivid memory of her was from an evening in 2007, when she was eight months pregnant with her second child. A number of activists were meeting at someone's home, discussing the women's movement, when a sharp knock came at the door. Uniformed police stormed in and began arresting the women present. One of the officers told Nasrin that they would not detain her and instructed her to go home. "I'm not going anywhere," she said to them. "My friends who you're taking away are my clients, and they're going to need me." She spent that night in a cold cell at the police station with her friends, who became instant clients, and defended them the next morning in court. She managed to secure their release that very day.

After 2009, Nasrin took on bolder cases. She represented Arash Rahmanipour, a young man who was arrested and later hanged for his alleged involvement in the Green Movement uprising. Nasrin discovered and made known that Rahmanipour had confessed only after Iranian authorities threatened his family.

Word reached me after her arrest that officials had promised to release her swiftly if she confessed to her alleged crimes and spoke out against me and other colleagues. If she did all this, they said, she would be reunited with her family.

After hearing this, I lay awake at night in my London apartment, staring at the shadows in the room, thinking about Nasrin. I thought about her children and how small they were, and about what I might have done myself, in her position.

In the end, she refused to capitulate, even though one of the intelligence agents told her, "I'll make sure that you stay in prison for over ten years, and that by the time you're released your three-year-old son will have grown into a man taller than you."

They refused to allow her to visit with her children and began summoning her husband for interrogation, threatening him with prosecution as well. But Nasrin stood firm. Some part of me had known she would. She is a slight woman, with deep brown eyes and bangs that slip over her face from under her head scarf. But she stood firm, and I worried for her, because she was inside the country, firmly within their grasp.

All of the lawyers who had been my colleagues at the center, my close friends and allies in our work, were now either in prison or in hiding. The state viewed them as guilty in their own right, for their own human rights work and the defense of their clients, but their ultimate guilt came from their association with me. Unable to snare me, the authorities had systematically tracked down and sentenced virtually every significant colleague I had worked with over the past decade. With Nasrin in prison, there was no one to defend my tax case. Other lawyers were frightened, certain that representing me would land them, too, in prison. Javad reached out to a few lawyers he knew personally, but each refused. I finally told him it was no use. No one was prepared to represent me, and even if we were to find someone, the court would not listen, anyway. My conviction would be reaffirmed at every stage.

When the Board of Settlement of Tax Disputes fi-

nally issued its verdict, the state moved to dispossess
me with an astonishing swiftness, perhaps the single
most efficient action committed by the Islamic Republic in the name of tax compliance. They put all my
properties up for sale within days, aided by already
having the deeds in their possession. It struck me that
back in August, when they'd freed Javad and asked him
for the deeds, this plan had already been under way;
they had known what would unfold, and had readied
themselves.

And with that, everything Javad and I had built and
earned together in the course of our thirty-five-year
marriage, except for our apartment, was seized. This
included the commercial flat that housed the center's
office and our orchard house and land outside Tehran.
These were all the fruits of forty years of hard work and
effort, aided in the last years by the Nobel Prize money
and some other awards I had received. While my own
work had been largely pro bono, Javad had spent a
career as a senior engineer and manager on some of
Tehran's most prominent construction projects. In the
safe-deposit box at Tejarat Bank that had ended up in
the midst of the controversy over my medal, I held
some family jewelry, a gold watch, and the diamond
ring Javad had given me when we married.

I never personally saw the notices printed in the national newspapers to sell my properties. Javad saw
them, as did my sister and brother, and I think of them
staring at the page, seeing that our lives had been put
up for sale.

In most such cases, the prices are set by an assessor, but what could I have expected? The authorities estimated the value of what I owned at laughably low prices—just a fraction of their actual value. The flat used by the Defenders of Human Rights Center was priced at $70,000, and our residential apartment was listed for around $200,000. Tehran real estate is some of the most expensive in the world. Those apartments, though modest, were in respectable, favored districts in north Tehran; they would have easily commanded several times that value. But the prices had their own logic. First, the revenue they raised would be insufficient to cover my tax debt, and I would remain, forever, a debtor to the government, my debt climbing each year. Second, these artificial prices would allow relatives or friends of the officials to snap up desirable flats for a fraction of their actual value. I knew one of the intelligence agents or their associates would be the buyers, and after the properties sold, I made inquiries and learned that both had been acquired by trusted government employees.

Soon it was the orchard's turn. When Javad and I bought the land, before the revolution, it was just an arid stretch on the outskirts of Tehran, the dirt rubbly and bare. We planted trees year after year, cherries and pomegranates, plums and walnuts, and in time the plot grew green and we began calling it the orchard. I could tell you how many feet separated the row of apricots from the pomegranates, and where near the southern edge the ground slopes down toward a brick wall. I can feel the smoothness of the wooden bench we bought the year Negar was born, and the spot on the back where the girls carved their initials into it, near a knot in the wood. I know the hour at dusk when the mosquitoes begin to buzz and hurl themselves toward the light, and the smell of night-blooming jasmine that hangs over the terrace. My children grew up in that orchard, it was where the family always gathered, and as Tehran became increasingly polluted and chaotic, it became the place I sometimes drove to just to breathe deeply. I could not permit that orchard to go to Mahmudi's cronies; it was just not in me to allow that.

I contacted some close friends in Tehran and asked them to bid on it at the public auction. I promised I wouldn't be upset if they became its owners, that I would view it as a great act of loyalty, actually. They agreed, and on auction day, the intelligence officials were surprised to see a crowd of bidders there, determined to secure the land. The price climbed a bit, but my friends managed to prevail in the end. When I heard the news, the only thing I could think was *When spring comes and the trees grow heavy with plums and cherries, I will never enjoy that sight again; but thank God my friends will eat that fruit, and not Mahmudi and his accomplices.*

Of the main bank account I held in my name, I managed to withdraw $50,000 through a third party who had power of attorney. But the rest, nearly the same amount, the officials confiscated to pay my debt. Once they sold everything off and seized all my ac-

counts, it became clear that the wholesale financial dispossession at the hands of the state still had not
generated enough money to pay my debts. In addition
to the standing charges against me for conspiring
against national security, I also became a formal debtor
to the Islamic Republic and, in absentia, was barred
from leaving the country. This means that if I ever go
back, my passport will be taken at the airport and I will
not be permitted to exit again. In the space of just one
year, the country whose justice system I had once represented at the highest level determined that I must be
a penniless traitor.

It began to rain softly as I reached my apartment building, pulling my grocery bags with me into the elevator.
It was one of those rare evenings when the city looked
as it did in old films, wreathed in fog that hovered
above the Thames, the sky and the air and the river
blending together in a bleak expanse of gray. I put some
tea on to brew—is there anything lonelier than brewing
a single teaspoon of loose tea for one person?—and sat
down to check my email, hoping to see a message from
one of my daughters.

Instead, the glowing screen showed a message from
Javad:

Mahmudi has told me that if I don't pass along
this message to you, he'll arrest me again. He in-

sists on speaking with you, and this is his mobile number.

I felt a burst of anger so strong it sent my pulse racing. I began to type quickly in reply:

I've read your message. And I know that before you read it, the agents will be reading it themselves. Tell Mahmudi for me that he's a nobody. If I want to speak to someone from intelligence, I'll speak to his boss's boss's boss. But if they want to speak to me, they have to prepare themselves to answer one question first: What law gives them the right to videotape someone's bed? If they can answer me this, I'm ready to speak to Mahmudi's boss's boss's boss.

After I sent that message—which, naturally, they read—this line of inquiry stopped. The intelligence agents realized that though they could interrogate my husband and my siblings and my friends, they would never establish a direct line to me. In the weeks that followed, I had a whole series of conversations with friends in Tehran, on lines that I knew were bugged. "Does Mahmudi think that if he gets a new ID card and passport he'll be clear?" I said. "I have his picture, and I've shared it with Interpol and every security agency in Europe. He can never set foot outside of Iran." I knew he preyed on fear. And though I was thousands of miles away, I could find ways to show him that I was not scared.

That spring, I lost my eyebrows. The culmination of Javad's arrest and everything they did to him, my sister's arrest, and then our final dispossession—all of this hurt me in ways I felt every day. And then slowly my eyebrow hairs started to fall out, until I was left with almost none, just a pale moon of forehead above my eyes.

I am not an especially vain person, but this bothered me as much as I imagine it would bother anyone else, losing an essential part of one's face. I used a pencil to color them back in, but every morning I would see myself in the mirror and feel that part of me had gone missing. And I suppose it had.

What the authorities in Iran had done to Javad, to our marriage, was something that could never be put right. Even if we learned to trust each other again and were able to forgive—how this could be accomplished if we were never able to see each other, I did not know—we would have permanently lost the goodness and purity of what we'd had before. I mean purity not in a moral sense but in terms of our ownership over our own story, our own history; our marriage was what we had built, a strong, loving bond forged over years of accommodation, a bond that had survived a revolution, a war, the loss of my career as a judge, the later regeneration of my professional life as a lawyer. That partnership was forever gone, and the question of what we might create in its place loomed. Javad still pursued his passport application through the various authorities, but so far he had met with little success. And though we still talked on the phone several times a week, the distance between us stretched wide.

I knew that one day the filmed confession would air, and finally that day came. In June, Iranian state television broadcast it on the prime-time flagship news program, *20:30,* named for the hour of the evening when most Iranians gathered around their televisions. The authorities wanted to reach the widest possible audience in order to tell them, *Look and see for yourself who your heroes really are; see how the West is interfering in our country's affairs.* The show it appeared on was prominent, always watched by Iranians who followed politics closely. As soon as they saw it, friends starting calling me. "Do you know this is happening?" everyone asked me. I thought it best not to embarrass Javad any further.

"Yes, I know. We both know everything."

Nargess saw it before me and rang, sobbing.

"We're humiliated," she repeated, over and over again.

"No, of course we're not. Only the Ministry of Intelligence is humiliated. They are, not us."

I didn't watch the confession. Friends recorded it for me, and later it emerged on YouTube. My assistant finally emailed me a link, and I realized I would have to see it sooner or later.

Even though I was prepared, this was one of my darkest hours. The authorities didn't air it as a straight confession; that would have been too ham-handed. Instead, they wove Javad's comments into a segment of news analysis that purported to examine the "real face" of one of the players of "political chess." What role was Shirin Ebadi playing? they asked. The segment showed me receiving the Nobel Peace Prize, but the announcer claimed that my activities were more like those of a political opposition figure. Because the piece was meant to be a historic overview, they included old photos of me and said that I had "managed to play a role in Iran's courts with the help of Ashraf Pahlavi's reforms." So my judgeship, reduced to "a role," was presented as having been enabled by the shah's sister; they superimposed my face on a glamorous photo of Ashraf Pahlavi, implying that I was a monarchist.

They said I had a grudge against the Islamic Republic that I was compelled to mention at every opportunity, and it was at that moment that they brought Javad onto the screen. The loss of my judgeship, he said, using crude terms he would never have uttered, "was such a blow that it gave her a complex against the Islamic Republic."

Anyone who knew Javad could feel him trembling inside, could see the tension in his frame and the way his hands fluttered awkwardly as he spoke. He cleared his throat every few seconds and spoke in the most unnatural way, repeating words randomly, as though dizzy. He wore a white shirt and looked as though he hadn't slept.

The narrative of the news segment was that I had received the Nobel Prize as part of a grand global conspiracy to undermine the Islamic Republic. This view they had to put in the mouth of my husband:

"Why did they give the prize to her? They wanted to give her an international standing, so that the Islamic Republic couldn't get in the way of her work. And they wanted to provide her with the funds to pay for that work. So she could work against the Islamic Republic."

The Nobel Prize, the voiceover noted, "has also been awarded to Shimon Peres and a number of other Zionists." And they made Javad say that I had taken on the Baha'is' case through some shady collaboration; I would defend the accused Baha'i leaders, and the community would try to make me "more famous internationally."

But the lowest point was when the presenter dropped his dripping tone of faux objectivity and turned openly tabloid. "And what's more, Shirin's husband moans about life with her," the voiceover said triumphantly.

Despite my international reputation, the script, as I recall it, had Javad saying, "In our house she couldn't even oversee the human rights of four people. I didn't even have the right to be in a bad mood. She fought with me often—once she broke my glasses, and on another occasion she tore my shirt. She would attack and hit me."

He went on: "We didn't have a good life together; it was one-sided. I had become Mr. Ebadi, my friends joked, saying that I had ended up with a husband rather than a wife."

And at the very end, he said this: "It is from this point that I feel I need to separate my path from hers."

When it was over, I thought, *This is what they do. They take the person you love the most away from you and crush them.* I looked curiously at the set they had constructed, the red sofa with wooden trim, the ugly beige satin curtains, the fake flowers on the table. Was that meant to be our home? Or where else was it meant to be? I felt a dull pain thudding in my temple, and tried to wipe out the image of that fake living room. In its place I had real memories: of us entertaining friends at the orchard, sitting around the old oak table, of the trip we took together to New York to see a fertility doctor, and how tightly we had held hands in the waiting room. I took a couple of pills for my headache and went and lay down on my bed. I closed my eyes, but sleep did not come.

Just in case anyone missed the segment, they aired it again a few days later. I don't know precisely what they were expecting from it, but it seemed to cause no ripples. The state television station had broadcast a number of forced confessions that same month, by other political prisoners. Iranians were growing to detest these show trials, these televised forced confessions; they found them reminiscent of the KGB, of North Korea, not worthy of Iran.

CHAPTER 18

The Spring That
Led to Winter

◆

In December 2010, a miracle happened in the Middle East. A miracle that started in Tunis, then grew and spread across the Arab world but never reached Iran. That was the month the people of Tunisia rose up and, within weeks, managed to oust their ruler.

I was transfixed by the news and started taking my tablet to bed with me, checking it before switching off the light and again first thing in the morning, to see whether there were any new developments in the tumult that was sweeping the region. The rumbling first spread to Egypt. In January 2011, Egyptians gathered in Cairo's Tahrir Square and began demanding that Hosni Mubarak step down. In those early days, the fast-moving events and the individuals who emerged to lead them sounded impressively inclusive and moderate, even the Islamists. Rashid al-Ghannushi, the leader of the Tunisian Islamists, who returned to his country after twenty-two years, announced, "I am neither Khomeini, nor the Taliban!" By this he meant he would not be seeking to bring Islamic fundamentalism to Tunisia. Even the Muslim Brotherhood in Egypt, for its part, called the protests a national uprising of the people of Egypt, both Muslims and Christians. The Islamic Republic of Iran watched these events with some nervousness, and then boldly declared the change sweeping the Arab world an "Islamic Awakening" inspired by Iran's own 1979 revolution.

Soon, in February 2011, it was the turn of Libya's Muammar Gadhafi, one of the region's most enduring and brutal leaders. Unlike Mubarak, Gadhafi held out stubbornly to the end, launching a killing campaign to crush those who opposed him. He would end up hiding in a drainpipe eight months later, and then be killed at close range.

For Iranians, it was an unsettling and emotional time. The first real shake-up in the region had started in Iran during the summer of 2009, after the stolen elections. At no time in the contemporary history of the Middle East, before that day in June 2009, had millions of people converged on the capital of a country in the region, demanding change. Although Iran's movement fizzled, crushed by the state and the chaotic, conflicting demands of its supporters, the first crackle, the first spark, had been Iranian. So it was painful for Iranians to see the upheaval and excitement in these neighboring Arab countries; if change was coming, why was it not Iran's destiny as well?

On February 9, less than two months after the start of Tunisia's revolt, the people of Tehran felt emboldened and applied for a permit to demonstrate in support of the Tunisian and Egyptian uprisings. For the regime, it was a sticky situation to handle; on the one hand, the Islamic Republic had supported the Arab uprising in the name of "Islamic Awakening," but on the other, they well knew that if Iranians were permitted to express their own solidarity and discontent, the implications for the regime could be dangerous.

The opposition leaders who had led the Green Movement, Mehdi Karroubi and Mir Hossein Mousavi, called for demonstrations, and even though the authorities refused to grant permission, Iranians came out into the streets anyway. Many were wounded, some were arrested, and some were killed. Six days later, people went back into the streets, and they were again crushed by the police. In Shiraz, security forces threw a university student off a bridge, killing him instantly. Scores were arrested there, too.

As students kept their protests going across the nation's universities, classes were canceled and the police stepped up their arrests. Those activists already in detention faced more severe restrictions and deteriorated conditions. Iran's largest cities, especially Tehran, were under total lockdown. Police in black riot gear lined key squares and public parks; police convoys hulked up and down the expressways. The state was taking no chances; it would not permit Iranians to seek the same freedoms the Tunisians and Egyptians had rallied for. The authorities moved to arrest Mousavi and Karroubi, the opposition leaders, tacitly admitting that the state was fearful enough about the prospect of a challenge that it had to arrest the key candidates in the most recent national election. No institution admitted responsibility for the arrests, but in interviews some Revolutionary Guards commanders and the intelligence minister suggested that the supreme leader had ordered everything personally.

In prison, even Mousavi and Karroubi's status as former senior officials did not secure them decent treatment. The authorities refused them regular visitation rights with family and kept them in secret apartments in undisclosed locations; they denied them access to the outdoors and adequate amounts of fruit and vegetables in their meals. Soon both fell ill, but even in the hospital, security officers lingered in their rooms day and night. At first, both men's wives stayed with them in detention, but after a few months, the authorities released Karroubi's wife. It was said that he preferred this, for he was a cleric and a traditional Muslim and felt aggrieved that the security agents often burst into the room without notice and would not even permit his wife to close the bathroom door when bathing.

The Western media labeled the uprisings taking place across the region the "Arab Spring." I do not know who coined this phrase, but it was a complete mistake. There was no spring. People's memories are very short, for anyone who knew the Middle East even a little would understand that a dictator's departure does not necessarily mean the end of dictatorship. Had everyone forgotten Iran in 1979 and the uprising that historians called the last great revolution of the twentieth century? How easily that dictator had been replaced by another, wearing different ideological robes. In my encounters with Arab friends, who were so overwhelmingly hopeful about the prospects for change, I did not wish to be the cynical Iranian. But I found the rise of the Islamists, who so promptly emerged from the shadows to seek power, deeply disturbing.

In both Egypt and Tunisia, the Islamists managed to take control through elections. The first thing they did after victory was to dampen their nations' feminist movements, through the approval of new laws justified in the name of sharia. These laws intensified the gender discrimination that already existed, and they also limited freedom of expression, so that the citizens would not dare express their dissatisfaction with them. The new rulers equated every single political criticism as criticism of Islam, and they labeled their critics "infidels."

The climate grew so extreme that in Tunis in October 2011, mobs attacked and threw firebombs at the home of a television station owner whose channel had aired *Persepolis,* an animated film based on the graphic novel by Marjane Satrapi documenting her coming-of-

age during Iran's Islamic Revolution. While the film
had nothing to do with Tunisia, it did powerfully convey the discontent of Iranian young people who'd lost
their cultural and social freedoms with the rise of the
country's new Islamist leaders. The Salafists, as the extreme Islamists in the Arab world are known, took issue
with a scene in the novel where Satrapi portrays God as
appearing in human form. On the surface, the Islamists were most incensed by this perceived violation—
strict, puritan Islam holds that images cannot be made
of God, the Prophet, or, indeed, any human or ani-
mal. But perhaps more important, the film carried a
powerful message about the vulnerabilities of a secu-
larist in the midst of an increasingly conservative revolution, and how quickly Islamists in power were able to
close up the space in which more liberal or secular
Middle Easterners used to exist. After the imam in a
downtown Tunis mosque railed against the film in his
sermon, thousands of Tunisians protested in the streets
and torched the television network's offices. The authorities prosecuted the television station's owner.

In Egypt, too, the presidential elections brought
into office an Islamist whose strict, power-grabbing
agenda soon caused great alarm. Mohamed Morsi, the
candidate of the Muslim Brotherhood, sought to re-
fashion Egyptian laws at home, limiting the democratic
process, while keeping the United States—a key donor
of foreign aid to Egypt—placated. When the people of
Syria rose up against their own dictator, Bashar al-
Assad, Morsi came out strongly in support of the op-

position and snubbed Iran, which was keen to rebuild the political ties with Egypt that had been severed after the 1979 revolution. But for Egyptians, Morsi's brief, one-year rule proved disastrous. Though he had promised a government "for all Egyptians," Morsi moved to strengthen his own Muslim Brotherhood party, granting himself far-ranging legal powers and trying to rush through a new draft constitution that liberals, many moderates, and Egypt's Coptic Christians opposed. When it came to women's rights, Morsi and the Muslim Brothers showed their intentions very quickly. They rejected a U.N. declaration condemning violence against women and explicitly said that wives should not be permitted to file complaints against their husbands for rape, adding that a husband should have "guardianship" over his wife.

These moves, especially the draft constitution, so infuriated Egyptians that they once again poured into Tahrir Square in protest, leading to days of unrest and mass demonstrations that culminated in clashes and, ultimately, the Egyptian military's removal of Morsi from power. There was a moment when the Egyptian president before the revolution, Hosni Mubarak, and the president after the revolution, Mohamed Morsi, both sat in prison watching the satire of the history of their country. The U.N. secretary-general and the head of the European Union asked the Egyptian military to release Morsi, and many observers in the West denounced his removal as a military coup.

But as an Iranian who had lived through a similar

history, I intimately understood and sympathized with the impulse that had led to the anti-Morsi demonstrations. What should a society do when a leader that is elected through a democratic process then seeks to subvert the very legal foundation on which the state, constitution, and electorate that voted him into power is based on? Can you allow a democratically elected leader to essentially destroy and subvert the principles that put him in power in the first place? Many Egyptians viewed Morsi's removal not as a subversion of democracy but an unfortunately necessary act that was required to safeguard it.

For me, it was almost a blow-by-blow reenactment of Iran's revolution, and I was relieved to see Egypt spared, to some extent, Iran's fate. In those early days of Egypt's uprising, in the first days of Morsi's presidency, I always felt anxious when I spoke to Arab friends, who were adamant that no one could snatch away the ideals of their revolution and that Morsi would not dare roll back the rights of Egyptian women. I wanted to say to them, "Look at me! I supported a revolution that ended up stripping me of my judgeship. I walked in the streets and chanted for freedom and helped a revolt that was seized by Islamists, leading to the collapse of my career, the collapse of the rights of women entirely." What a bitter, startling time it was for me, to watch all this unfolding in the region, and to hear the indignation of Western liberals, who felt it was "undemocratic" for Egyptians to stop Morsi and the Muslim Brotherhood from taking over Egypt.

So the tumult of 2011, despite all the hope and promise of those dramatic moments, did not bring about a spring of any sort for the Arab world. And in Iran, not only was there no sign of spring at all; the citizens lived in a permanent winter. With the imprisonment of the key opposition leaders Mousavi and Karroubi, the majority of Iranians who had held out hope that eventually, with time, the system would reform itself from within lost hope. And, disturbingly, around the same time, the most regressive forces calling for regime change in Iran gained ground in the West. The Mojahedin-e Khalq Organization, which had emerged before the 1979 Iranian revolution but had transformed itself over time into an armed resistance group, began drawing the attention and support of members of the U.S. Congress and some prominent former officials. Washington had long designated the MKO as a terrorist group, but in September 2012 the group won; the State Department took it off its list of designated terrorist organizations. Iranians across the world widely rejected this group—if there was anything that Iranians of various political stripes agreed on, it was this, for the members of the MKO had joined Saddam Hussein's forces during the Iran-Iraq War, fighting against their own countrymen. So it was particularly jarring and worrisome to see mainstream U.S. politicians cozying up to the MKO, even if only to needle the Islamic Republic.

Around the same time, a palpable swell of affection was growing around Reza Pahlavi, the eldest son of the

last shah, whom monarchists considered the rightful
king of Iran. For years, Pahlavi had been politically active from his base in Washington, D.C., though it neither seemed that he was a natural leader for an
opposition movement nor that Iranians were particularly interested in reestablishing the monarchy. But at
a time when the political situation in Iran looked terribly bleak and Iranians increasingly felt that the supreme leader was not willing to retreat at all, Reza
Pahlavi seemed to be a figure that a measure of hope
and support could coalesce around.

In April 2011, the husband of one of my closest
friends, Mehrangiz Kar, jumped off his Tehran apartment building. Like me, Mehrangiz was a lawyer, and
she had dedicated the years after the Iranian revolution
to writing about the law, about legal discrimination. We
were family friends—I had watched her daughters grow
up alongside my own—and, like me, Mehrangiz had
spent time in Evin Prison. Her crime had been attending a conference in Berlin during the presidency of
Mohammad Khatami, and for this she served fifty days.

Sometime after her release, Mehrangiz was diag-
nosed with breast cancer. She traveled abroad for treatment, and while she was outside Iran, the authorities
arrested her husband, Siamak Pourzand; they had previously arrested him on various occasions and forced
him to confess on television to things he did not believe and crimes he had not committed. And as with

Javad, the confession did not ultimately secure him freedom from torment.

Because Siamak fell ill in prison, the authorities eventually agreed that he could serve the rest of his sentence under house arrest. Months passed, and Siamak languished in the confines of his prison-house, unable to see his wife, who could not travel back to Iran without fear for his safety, and his daughters. He grew increasingly depressed, until one night he threw himself off his apartment building; he died instantly. The night after his death, I watched his daughter Leily, whom I had known when she was a little girl in ponytails, speak about her father on television. Her eyes were swollen from crying, and her voice was raw. "My father courageously chose death, a kind of death that would expose the injustice that was inflicted on him," she said.

Leily's maturity and her pain, the sadness in her face, made me cry. I sat on my sofa thinking of the families, my own and others, torn apart and brutalized by the Islamic Republic. Since childhood, Leily had watched her parents go in and out of prison, her adolescence cast in a halo of anxiety caused by security officials. I thought of my own daughters, and how the paths we had chosen as parents had rushed them too soon into adulthood, imposed on them the sort of worry and anxiety that should only be the burden of adults. In the shadows of my living room, I watched the lights of the city flicker in the distance, and I imagined how bright the night sky would look if every one of the Islamic Republic's victims shone as a separate star.

◆ ◆ ◆

It was a cloudy February day—Valentine's Day, I realized, seeing all the chocolates and flowers in the shop windows as I walked through Cambridge. I was moving slowly, taking in the cobblestones and the rusty-red bricks of the university buildings, watching the joggers muffled in gloves and hats speed past, the students walking and laughing in small packs. I was thinking about Javad. Though I was still feeling raw over what had happened, the girls and I missed him, especially when we were together. My daughter Negar and her husband, Behnood, had moved to Boston some months earlier, to take up postdoctoral fellowships at MIT and Harvard, respectively. I had come to visit because Negar was having a baby, and one of the very few wishes I've had all of my adult life, to hold my grandchild in my arms, was finally coming true.

For weeks Javad had been chasing his passport, so that he could be there for the baby's birth. But at every turn, Mahmudi had been waiting and finding ways to block him. His application for a new passport, to replace the doctored and ruined one he had received back after getting out of prison, had been rejected.

At the passport office, Javad had received a reference number with which to follow up his case, and the trail led to the court that was imposing a ban on his freedom of movement. There, he learned that his name was included in the case that had been brought against me for "conspiring against national security."

"I'm listed as your 'collaborator,' " he told me on the phone one night. "The judge read to me from the document he had; it said that allowing me to leave the country 'would not be in the interest of security.' "

The judge who'd issued the order told Javad frankly that as long as Mahmudi did not withdraw the restriction, nothing could be done to secure him the right to travel. With Negar's due date approaching, Javad had become desperate. He still saw Mahmudi regularly for his monthly or twice-monthly interrogation sessions, and recently Mahmudi had taken to standing him up. Javad would wait for hours in a corridor or reception room, only to be told at the end of the day that he would need to return the next day, that Mahmudi had been too busy to see him.

"They do this—it's their game," I told Javad. "They're trying to hurt you and frustrate you psychologically." I wanted to soothe him, but privately I did not understand what it was that they wanted from him. He had confessed on film, and they knew very well that he was completely at their mercy. So what was the game now?

One afternoon, Javad asked Mahmudi directly to lift his travel ban.

"My eldest daughter is giving birth to her first child, and I'd like to be there," he said. "She has no other family in America, and she asks me every time we speak whether I can make it."

Mahmudi rubbed his stubble, his brown eyes glinting.

"Why doesn't your wife shut up?"

"She doesn't listen to me. As you well know."

"Man, why do you want a wife who doesn't listen to you? If she loved you, she'd pipe down for your sake, at least. She knows full well that she's not going to overthrow this regime and that nothing is going to change around here. But she insists on carrying on, even though she knows her silence would fix all your problems."

Javad didn't reply. And in the end, he was unable to leave the country.

So I was alone with Negar in Boston, and the evening we got Javad's news that he would not be allowed to travel, I helped her as she wrapped her baby boy, Radean, in a flannel blanket, placed a small patchwork bear next to him in his bassinet, and made a short film to send to her father. I stayed with Negar for about two months. Often during the day I would hold Radean and sway back and forth in the living room, so Negar could catch up on her sleep. The apartment was frequently silent during the day, as Negar napped and Radean breathed softly in my arms. His breath smelled sweet, like milk.

Mahmudi slammed the door of the interrogation room so hard the tea on his desk sloshed in its cup. The room was the same as ever: stark white walls that looked gray in the fluorescent light, two wooden chairs, the stained brown schoolroom carpet. But on the table, Javad noticed, were more folders than usual. This made him hopeful.

Norouz, the first day of spring and the start of the Persian New Year, was approaching, and Javad was back again with Mahmudi, seeking permission to travel so he could join the rest of us in Boston. My daughter Nargess and I were flying from London to visit Negar, and though we had not asked Javad to come—it seemed cruel to continually invite him, knowing he was unable to travel—when he'd heard about our plans, he'd decided to try one more time to get his travel ban lifted. This time, he'd changed his tack. A friend's brother had a position in the Ministry of Intelligence and had made a direct appeal to Mahmudi on Javad's behalf.

"So here we are," Mahmudi said, tapping a pen against the files. "Back to the same question."

Javad waited, folding his hands in his lap. Being quiet seemed the best way to avoid antagonizing the interrogator. Mahmudi held the pen up to the light, examining it.

"I'm going to allow you to go, just this once. But you have to return quickly, in less than a month. When you get back, you come here and sign an affidavit vowing that you said nothing against the Islamic Republic while abroad."

"Of course, and can I just say—"

"I'm not finished," Mahmudi interrupted. "You leave your apartment as collateral, and if we see anything we don't like, it becomes ours. And you also have to carry this pen with you at all times. It's a fountain pen with a built-in GPS, so we'll be able to monitor you at all times and know where you're going."

He again held up the pen, the same one he had been playing with since he'd walked into the room, and twirled it in his fingers. The apartment we owned in Yusef Abad, our home, was the only property that had not been confiscated and sold off to pay the tax penalties. Mahmudi knew it was the only security, both financial and emotional, we had left.

Javad thanked him and left quickly, before Mahmudi could change his mind or think of something else to complicate matters. But once Javad got home, he rang his friend and asked if his brother in the intelligence ministry could mediate with Mahmudi to have the tracking pen demand withdrawn. In the end Mahmudi agreed, but he still took the property deed to Javad's apartment as collateral, to be forfeited if he did not return to Iran within one month.

Your children do not stop being your children when they become adults. When Javad and I were finally reunited in Boston that March, after nearly three years, I was deeply aware of our daughters watching us, anxious. It was Norouz, the most important holiday for us as Iranians, and Negar had a new baby. But the first day I saw Javad, I kept darting into the kitchen, to make tea, or into the bathroom, to compose myself. I held my grandson for hours that day, cuddling him and pretending to be calm.

That wasn't my husband out there in the living room; it was just a shell of him, a broken man. He looked about a decade older, with more lines etched on his face, and there was a bitter cast to his features that never lifted. He had once been a charming man; he used to smile broadly and often, his eyes brightening with the witty jokes and asides that came naturally to him. I had always appreciated that quality of his—the way he energized a room and drew people to him. But now he would sit in a corner for hours, without saying a word. Even around the dinner table when we were all laughing or reminiscing about something, he had a distracted, faraway look, as though part of him was somewhere else. He was polite to me but colder, and I could feel the girls watching and noticing. I also felt a gaping distance between us. Before he'd arrived, our phone conversations had been growing shorter and chillier. It was as though we had nothing in common anymore, nothing to talk about.

Late one day we went out for a walk together, up and down the streets of Negar's Boston neighborhood, with the trees still bare and the afternoon light waning. Near a park, Javad stopped.

"Didn't you always say that human rights start from one's own family?" he asked me. "When you noticed that one of your colleagues wasn't paying enough attention to their partner or their kids, didn't you always tell them that family always comes first? I just want to know why you were not prepared to practice what you preach."

There were some benches in the park, and though it was cold, we sat down.

"More than twenty-five years have passed since you

started your human rights work," he said. "Has anything positive happened in all this time? Have you
achieved anything? If you helped get ten prisoners released, twenty more immediately took their place. Have
you brought freedom to Iran?"

My whole body froze up as he spoke. I didn't interrupt, just perched on the bench, listening to him.

"If you're fair," he went on, "you'll admit that all
your efforts have been in vain. And that all you've succeeded in doing is bringing misery upon yourself and
your family."

I didn't know what to say to him. I could see clearly
how tired and fed up he was, how Mahmudi's persecution and the hounding of the intelligence agents had
blackened his life. He was yearning for peace and calm,
and I did not blame him for that for a second. But I was
almost sixty-five years old, and I couldn't just change
my ideas and my values, or the way I lived. I couldn't
abandon everything I had worked for throughout most
of my life, or abandon my colleagues who were sitting
in prison. I couldn't sit in some remote corner of the
world and stop being who I was. I felt dizzy and disconnected, having this conversation with my husband of
almost four decades in a Boston park. I rubbed my
hands together to warm them up, and watched a gar-
bage truck rumble to a stop in front of a row of houses.

"I don't want to say that I don't have any answers," I
slowly told him. "But for me, all I can say is that nothing is going to change."

He looked at me for a long time. I will never in all

my years forget that spring day that was still cold and
frozen with winter. That day a well of guilt sprang up
inside me that I immediately understood I would carry
forever. Until that day I had never done anything that
had made me feel guilt. Everything until that point had
been shared between us; my work and its impact on our
life had been something that evolved slowly, and even
during the worst of times, Javad had stood by me. When
the mob came to attack our building, he was the one
who went downstairs and stood up to the rioters and
challenged the police to protect us. He had never es-
poused all my ideals, but he had remained steadfast. It
had always been clear that the guilt and blame lay with
the government, and that I wasn't the one hurting us.

All of that understanding seemed dated now; all that
mattered was the hurt in my husband's broken face. To
all my other pains and sorrows, I now added this, the
end of my marriage. I was deeply wounded, but I knew
that if we stayed together the authorities would perse-
cute Javad forever. Though I could have put up a fight,
I understood that ending our marriage was the only
way I could truly protect him.

Javad stayed in Boston with us for three weeks, then
went on to Canada to visit his sister. He returned to
Iran before the end of the appointed month, so that he
could retain the only property he now had left in the
world and get his ownership deed back.

I returned to Europe and decided to expand my activities. I wanted to establish and register a nonprofit organization that could serve as a hub and center for all of my various human rights work. After consulting with a few lawyers, I chose London as my base, and around the end of 2013 I registered the Centre for Supporters of Human Rights. When I helped found this center, I wanted to focus its work tightly on Iran and the right to legally defend those accused of crimes of conscience. The Iranian lawyers who worked so tirelessly to represent political prisoners were extraordinarily vulnerable. The authorities monitored them closely, imprisoned scores of them, and intimidated their relatives. The Iranian Bar Association, under pressure from the Ministry of Intelligence, did not bother to defend its members harassed in this way. So at the outset of founding this new network, I dedicated our attention to defending these lawyers and to reporting the troubles they faced to the United Nations and to the International Bar Association.

In time, working with a number of lawyers who had left Iran in the aftermath of the 2009 protests, we created a vibrant network connecting lawyers inside and outside the country; we collaborated when possible on human rights cases, training workshops, and publishing legal articles. This sort of connectivity was uplifting and motivating for both the lawyers forced into exile and the lawyers working away inside Iran.

Throughout all of this, my business didn't prevent me from staying in touch with Javad. But each time we spoke, I found him colder and more distant than the time before. Most of our conversations revolved around our daughters: their work, Negar's new family, and Nargess's studies. We had nothing else to talk about anymore.

Then one day Javad told me that he wanted to separate. If we were divorced he might finally rid himself of Mahmudi, and he might also want to marry again. Had I expected this? If I am honest, I would say I don't really know. I knew that he had every right to enjoy a normal life, rather than the kind that had been inflicted on him the past four years. I told him that I, too, agreed, and we decided that I should give him power of attorney to go to court and pursue the legal formalities for a divorce. Of course, under Iranian law he didn't need my agreement to divorce me, but my formal authorization would make things much easier.

Part of being an exile, a nomad, is that the most significant moments in your life pass by in places where you have no memories and no past. On a warm, summery day, I was in Madrid to speak at the Fifth World Congress Against the Death Penalty. But my thoughts were trained on what I was about to do as I entered the Iranian embassy, which was housed in a hacienda-style building of white stucco and brick. I passed through the lacy black lattice gates, carrying the certified power-of-attorney letter I had written, authorizing divorce proceedings. The embassy staff stamped it with the official seal, and I went directly to the post office to send it to Javad. Then I gave a talk about the death penalty, during which I explained how in authoritarian countries the practice is exploited by the state to execute activists and, often, minors.

The following day, June 12, 2013, Iranians would vote in their next presidential election, the second vote I would be missing. Strikingly, I had also been in Spain, in Majorca, four years earlier, on the eve of the last presidential election. Four years earlier, just as today, my destiny had taken a sharp turn. Last time, events had unfolded in a way that would keep me permanently outside of my homeland. This time, it was the ending of my thirty-seven-year marriage.

Even when both parties agree to a divorce, it is still a distressing and dark time. I didn't regret what I had done, especially since Javad had initiated the divorce himself. But for a long while, I felt myself walking through a great, stretching emptiness. When I passed the men's cologne section of duty-free shops, I felt a stab of sadness, remembering how I was always the one to buy Javad his colognes from the airport. At random points I would be accosted by memories: of the day we planted the first tree in the orchard, or of how lovingly Javad dealt with one of the girls' scraped knees. Now there was no one to ask whether I was eating properly. There was no one who understood me so intimately, who knew the kinds of jokes that made me laugh most or the blend I liked in loose tea. In Madrid, I kept myself busy with meetings and told myself I had to overcome my grief. I know I shouldn't let depression get the better of me.

This is why I intensified my work in the newly formed CSHR, to make sure that every single day I remembered that I had been born in a country where a mere intelligence agent had the power to crush a person's life. I needed to remember that it was no good to keep looking behind myself and that I should instead look only ahead, at the future.

What helped me overcome some of that sorrow at the time was the news Nargess, my younger daughter, gave me. She told me she had found the man she wanted to spend her life with and that she had agreed to marry him. One evening we had dinner together, and she introduced her fiancé, Ali, to me. He belonged to a cultured Iranian middle-class family and had a master's degree in computer science from a prominent British university. He was working in London for a governmental organization and was three years older than Nargess. I felt that he would make a suitable partner, and I gave them my blessing. They began planning their wedding, to be held in London that August.

They had decided to get married at city hall, but I also wanted them to have an Islamic ceremony, because of our faith. I went to see an Iranian cleric in London— most of the Shia clerics in London are Iranian—and explained the situation.

"I want to have the Koranic marriage sura read for my daughter," I said.

"Will both you and her father be present?" he asked.

I told him that her father was in Iran and wouldn't be able to attend, but that it wouldn't be an issue, because we were not looking to take the marriage certificate to the Iranian embassy. "We just want an Islamic ceremony," I said.

"Well, then I can't do it. Iranian law doesn't allow that," he said imperiously, drawing his robes together. "I don't want a certificate like that going to the embassy."

"But we don't want it to go to the embassy!" I protested, exasperated. "We're Muslims, and we want an Islamic ceremony. This is just for us."

After the revolution, Iranian family law became based on sharia, and the judiciary decreed that when a woman is getting married for the first time, she requires the permission of her father. Even if she is fifty years old and happens to be a minister in the government. If the father is not present or does not agree, the woman is obliged to go to court and request special permission to marry. This medieval law applies only to women, of course, and it creates ridiculous amounts of trouble in Iran. Iranian men can marry whomever they want from the age of fifteen on, but a fifty-year-old woman needs permission.

"Where in Islam is it written that this is required?" I asked the cleric. "It's not in the Koran. The source is a very weak passage, and there are many other sources that carry more weight, theologically."

"The Islamic Republic doesn't allow it, and I don't want any trouble."

"To hell with you, if you don't know Islam. I know Islam better than you do, and you know very well that we don't need you, as a cleric, to perform it."

I was more saddened than angry. I was more of a Muslim than he was, and I knew the tenets of Islam far better than this man who wore clerical robes and claimed the title of emissary of our faith. And so I performed Nargess's marriage ceremony myself, reading the Koranic verses for them at home without any fanfare.

I was glad to see Nargess leaving to live at her husband's home, and I felt grateful that she was starting a life she wanted, and that I would be around to watch it grow and flourish. One of my great sorrows was that my life had changed Nargess's destiny. Her plan in life had been to become a lawyer, and through great effort she had studied the law in Iran, passed her initial exam, and completed her internship. All she had needed to secure her license was to pass the final bar exam. She should have sat for the exam in 2009, but because she had been sorting out her PhD applications, she'd submitted a letter asking to postpone her exam by a year. The Iranian Bar Association had refused to accept her letter, on the grounds that her mother had been disbarred.

I felt that my work, and the harassment it prompted from the intelligence ministry, had destroyed Nargess's chances of practicing law in Iran. But she felt differently and often said so. She said she could make more of a difference working outside Iran, raising awareness of all the rights violations inside the country. She often reminded me of what she'd been like as a child, chafing at the restrictions and desperate to leave Iran. One post on her blog was about how living outside Iran had made her appreciate Ramadan again. Unlike me, she didn't blame Mahmudi for her fate.

But as pleased as I was about Nargess starting her new life with her husband, I was also weighed down by a heavy sorrow. It had now been over four years since I'd left my homeland, a place I loved passionately, a place that inspired and motivated me and formed much of my very identity. I was away from all my closest friends, as well as all the colleagues and associates I had worked with so intimately over the years. Fate had cast me, alone, into a land whose culture I didn't understand adequately, and whose language I could not speak especially well, either. My daughters now had their own lives, and I had separated from my husband. Javad and I still spoke on the phone occasionally, and he was still the one I turned to when I needed something from Iran. He sent me books and, each Norouz, a calendar to help me chart my year. But these small kindnesses did not fill the long hours that stretched around me. After each long day at work, I spent most of my evenings alone at home. I wasn't in the mood to accept the invitations of the large group of acquaintances I'd made. I wanted my old friends, but they weren't here. I had become deeply lonely.

In all divine religions, there is an unalterable constant, and that is the loneliness of God Almighty. In other words, there is only one single God, who has no partner or colleague. Whenever I felt sad, a philosophical question always came to my mind: "Is God happy to be alone?"

CHAPTER 19

Bloodbath as Lesson

♦

One autumn day during his second term, President Mahmoud Ahmadinejad traveled to the village of Bint Jbeil, in southern Lebanon, and waved an Iranian flag just a few miles away from the border with Israel. He addressed a thronging crowd in the same stadium where Hezbollah leader Hassan Nasrallah gave his victory speech to mark Israel's withdrawal from occupied southern Lebanon in 2000. The region is still one of the most tense stretches of border anywhere in the world, with Israeli snipers watching through the crosshairs of high-powered rifles and Hezbollah fighters scouring for opportunities to kidnap a soldier.

In this distant fight, Iran is a key player. As a backer and funder of Hezbollah, it shares in the militia's victories and funds its losses. The Israeli-Lebanon war of

2006, often called the Hezbollah war, resulted in the leveling of nearly 90 percent of the buildings in Bint Jbeil. The sleepy village lined with cedar trees was turned to rubble, and it was Iranian money that paid for its resurrection. Tehran paid for new apartment buildings, hospitals, and schools, and now Ahmadinejad was enjoying the adulation and gratitude of the Lebanese who'd benefited. Photos of the Ayatollah Khomeini covered the stadium walls, alongside images of Hezbollah heroes, and the flags of the Islamic Republic, Hezbollah, and the Lebanese state fluttered together.

For Iran, Lebanon, Hezbollah, and the gateway through which it funnels all its money, arms, and military support—the neighboring state of Syria—are no small investment. These alliances are central to Iran's projection of influence in the region, and they also provide a convenient theater through which Iran can teach its own citizens a lesson about what happens when a people rise up. By now, we are used to images of the Syrian civil war, one of the greatest humanitarian tragedies of our young century. We have come to know that it is a bloody internal conflict, pitting Sunni Syrians against the regime of Bashar al-Assad, who is an Alawite; the Alawite sect is a branch of Shia Islam. But before Syria's conflict became a civil war, it was a broad-based uprising against the tyranny of Assad. It was Assad, with the support of his Iranian backers, who turned an essentially democratic revolt into a sectarian war. The Iranian leadership backed him in this effort, with a close eye trained on the Iranian homeland, a thousand miles away.

Through the bloodbath that unfolded in Syria, the Islamic Republic conveyed a clear warning to Iranians, both those inside the country and the opposition movement abroad. The message was: If you rise up, we will crush you. We will not retreat a single step. We will not be Hosni Mubarak of Egypt, who stepped down. We will be Assad, who would rather torch his country to the ground than relinquish power. The fate of Iran will be the fate of Syria.

Iranians had not been harboring dreams of violently overthrowing their government. But the Syrian case unfolded during a specific and uncertain time for Iran, directly between the 2009 uprising and the 2013 presidential election, a time when Iranians were weighing the prospect of change, observing the hopeful changes in other parts of the region, and considering how their own regime might be transformed. The lessons of 2009 were painful, and the destruction of Syria playing out every night on Iranians' televisions was an intimate reminder of how the Islamic Republic would respond, should Iranians seek change through the streets. This, I believe, is what prodded people to start thinking about internal reforms once again, despite their abject failure in recent years. There seemed to be no choice but to seek gradual improvements through the current system. This is why so many Iranians were prepared to vote again in 2013, putting aside the bitter memories of the 2009 election.

In the run-up to the 2013 vote, the Iranian regime was careful to avoid the mistake of 2009, and the state vetting body approved only candidates who would be unconditionally and unquestionably obedient to the supreme leader. No more Mousavis and Karroubis, leaders who might go maverick and challenge the system. Each and every candidate had to have a proven track record of unwavering political loyalty; they had to be the sort of men who didn't mind dissimulation and were comfortable speaking out against their true positions when required. The vetting was tough enough that Akbar Hashemi Rafsanjani, the old stalwart of Islamic Republic politics, who had led Iran through two terms as president after the end of the war with Iraq, was disqualified as a candidate. It was a vote that more than anything underscored the now explicit and all-encompassing power of the supreme leader.

One prerequisite for running seemed to be speaking out on record against the 2009 *fitna,* or conspiracy, as the hard-line establishment had termed the Green Movement uprising. The reformists at first considered making their election participation contingent on Mousavi and Karroubi's release from house arrest, though later they shifted course and agreed to field a candidate. None of their picks secured clearance, however, so they backed Hassan Rouhani, a moderate conservative who in the world of Iranian politics had long been comfortably considered part of the conservative elite. He had held numerous senior security positions over the years but was seen as being a pragmatist rather than a right-wing Islamist ideologue.

On the election trail, Rouhani sounded more progressive than someone of his political stripe and began attracting the attention of the moderate middle class, who would have ordinarily backed a reform candidate. During one of the televised debates between the candidates, he argued that Iran shouldn't pursue a nuclear program at the expense of everything else that mattered to people's livelihoods. "It is very good for the [uranium enrichment] centrifuges to turn," he said, "but the wheels of the country must also turn."

In June 2013, Iranians took to the polls under sunny, bright skies to again vote for president. They did this as an act of faith, hoping that the system would not tamper with their votes, as it did in 2009, and would allow them the freedom to choose their elected leader, as the Islamic Republic's constitution, for all its flaws, provides for. The favored candidate of the establishment was a dour old negotiator, Saeed Jalili, but in the days before the election, an outpouring of frustration and discontent broke out around the status quo Ahmadinejad had created. Significantly, it was not just ordinary Iranians who were furious but also many stalwart regime figures who were themselves participating in the election. The supreme leader's old foreign policy adviser, Ali Akbar Velayati, and nearly all of the other candidates used the televised national debates to lambast Ahmadinejad's foreign and economic policies. It was finally clear and exposed on national television, and upheld by senior regime figures, that Ahmadinejad had steered Iran to the brink of war and economic collapse.

Since I spoke to my friends and relatives in Iran every day, I knew well how high inflation and the collapse of Iran's currency, the *rial,* were destroying people's quality of life. Many of my daughters' friends who had left Iran to study abroad had been forced to return home, as the *rial* had lost nearly half of its value in two weeks of 2012. The situation was so bad that Iran, once a wealthy country, owed money to the World Bank, and its inflation rate hovered around 50 percent. The United States' sanctions had also contributed to the economy's deterioration, hindering trade and choking Iran off from the international banking system.

Naturally, the candidate who sounded the most pragmatic, who spoke of hope and moderation, who promised to fix the economy and repair Iran's relationship with the West would generate the most popularity. This man was Hassan Rouhani, and he made a key the symbol of his campaign. He would unlock all the doors for Iran, he vowed, and bring the nation back into the world. He won resoundingly.

The day the authorities announced the results, Iranians celebrated in the streets, pouring into parks on foot and cruising in automobiles up and down Teh-

ran's major boulevards, honking their horns. Strikingly, some chanted the slogan "Thank you, dictator!"
With this they were conveying to the supreme leader
how much they resented his authoritarian rule but, at
the same time, showing their gratitude for having their
votes respected.

For me, watching from afar, it was a bittersweet moment: Iranians' demands for free, democratic elections had been so far reduced, their expectations so
diminished, that they were gladdened by vote count-
ing that was not fraudulent, in an election process
that had vetted candidates so stringently that it could
hardly be considered a competition. This change was
the very outcome the political system had been seeking.
Through the brutal crackdown in 2009, Iranians' aspirations for democratic change had been crushed,
and in their place the people had acquiesced to the
state's rigid, controlled handover of the presidency to
one of the few men it had deemed sufficiently loyal.

It only took as many days as Rouhani needed to ap-
point his cabinet for it to become clear that he was not
the leader people had imagined. His choice for justice
minister was one of the clerics reportedly implicated
in the execution of political prisoners in 1988, in
which an estimated total of 4,500 citizens were killed.
When I had represented the family of Dariush and
Parvaneh Forouhar, dissident intellectuals who'd
been stabbed to death in their home in 1998, the
cleric's name had come up repeatedly, invoked by
the agents accused of carrying out the killings. At the

same time, the supreme leader kept insisting in his public speeches that Iran would not be compromising on any of its policies, either foreign or domestic.

And what of Ahmadinejad? The ex-president, who'd had some serious disagreements with the supreme leader during his second term in office, once again became the focus of attention after declaring his support for the leader. That same summer of Rouhani's election, the supreme leader appointed Ahmadinejad to the powerful Expediency Council, which is charged with mediating disputes between the parliament and the Guardian Council. Therefore, although everyone had thought that Ahmadinejad's political career was over, he had in effect started a new era, and is believed to have received his reward for remaining aligned with the supreme leader. Ahmadinejad's "invaluable efforts" during his time as president, the supreme leader said, had earned him a place at the helm of one of the state's most influential bodies. It was an early signal that while Ahmadinejad had been shifted out of the limelight, his radical positions were still shared by the highest authorities. In the meantime, Mousavi and Karroubi were still under house arrest, and hundreds of others who had ended up incarcerated because of the 2009 presidential elections were still languishing in prisons.

The Iranian state, as ever, is extremely adept at hiding the costs of its various policies from its citizens. Ayatollah Khomeini's favorite expression after the 1979 revolution was that the "the Islamic Revolution must be exported beyond Iran's borders." In the intervening years, the precise meaning and impulse behind that view has become clear. It drives Iran's arming and support for Hezbollah, through which Iran extends its influence throughout the Levant and to the very borders of Israel. It drives Iran to create instability in corners of the region as far-flung as Yemen, aiding the country's Shia rebels. Those with longer memories will, of course, recall the Mykonos incident, when Iran dispatched assassins to execute Iranian activists in a German restaurant. The cases are myriad. Iran has sent arms to Gambia, confiscated off the coast of Nigeria. And, more recently, there is the suppurating civil war in Syria, a conflict that has made four million Syrians refugees. This conflict is abetted by Iran, which is bolstering its ally Bashar al-Assad, bent on retaining its supply route to Syria and beating back the Sunni extremists that, incensed by Iran's backing of Shia forces in Iraq, have essentially opened a wider front against Iran. All of this shows the legacy of Khomeini's bid to "export" the revolution, which in practice has meant that Iran has used and continues to use any means and resources to advance its international influence, regardless of what interference this poses in the affairs of other countries.

What I believe has slowly become clear to the people of the world, especially Muslims, is that Iran waves the banner of Palestinian solidarity chiefly to promote its own interests. When Palestinian leader Mahmoud Abbas asked the U.N. General Assembly to admit Palestine to the United Nations, Ayatollah Khamenei denounced him as a traitor; with such a request, Iran's supreme leader argued, Abbas was accepting the legitimacy of Israel. Palestine is the golden cause of the Islamic Republic, the center of its claim that it defends the Muslims of the world. But what about the massacre of Muslims of Chechnya or the ruthless killing of the Uighur Muslims in China? Iran has said little, if anything, about these abuses because Russia and China are firm supporters, willing to defend Iran's nuclear ambitions as part of their own chess game with the United States.

Such double standards and hypocrisies reveal Iran's political ambitions and underscore what an enormous challenge President Rouhani has before him. The Islamic Republic's foreign policy and modus operandi in the world are largely based on negative influence: the arming of proxies, the nurturing of militias, and investment in Shia soft power; it will take a wholesale realignment of the regime's perception of its interests to change this. But change it must. In the long term, a state that brokers its power in the shadows cannot be on sound enough terms with the world to provide security for its citizens. Under Ahmadinejad, Canada and Britain severed their ties with Iran, and the Sunni-ruled countries of the region, particularly Bahrain, the United Arab Emirates, Kuwait, and Saudi Arabia, view Iran with great trepidation and hostility. Indeed, Saudi Arabia's rivalry with Iran is slowly eroding the region from within, with proxy conflicts emerging in Iraq and

Syria, and a dangerous sectarian strife is stoking instability and religious hatred where even just five years ago
there had been peace and coexistence. This is perhaps
the most troubled, dangerous time in the modern history of the region.

Having inherited a system that thrives by sowing
chaos in the region, Rouhani will have to decide how
far he wants to try to go. A genuine first step would be
abandoning Iran's support for Assad in Syria, but Iran
may countenance such a move only when it truly sees
no other way out. Sadly, despite the destruction of
Syria, the leveling of the city of Aleppo, and the giant
migration of Syria's population, we are not there yet.

The easier space, one might say, for Rouhani to
bring about change is internally. How the Iranian government treats its own citizens is a private affair, unaf-
fected by the militias roaming across Iraq or the ups
and downs of the nuclear negotiations. Since 2009,
violations of human rights in Iran have intensified
markedly, and the United Nations has designated a
"special rapporteur" for Iran, whose reports detail the
gravity of what is happening inside the country.

As for the discriminatory laws themselves—the whole
legal structure through which the Islamic Republic en-
shrines gender discrimination and violent punish-
ments, including lashing and stoning—Rouhani can
have little impact. The laws can be changed only by the
parliament, whose deputies are vetted through the
Guardian Council. So despite having a pragmatist in

office once again, Iran remains a country where a man can marry up to four wives, where women face enormous challenges securing a divorce, and where a married woman cannot travel without the written permission of her husband. The list of discriminatory laws that are unfit for Iran's modern society is long, and if we are blunt about it, Hassan Rouhani stands no chance of bringing about reforms in this area.

What he has a better chance of success with is tackling the human rights violations that are not legally based but arise from the repressive ways the authorities treat Iranian citizens. Here I mean the late-night raids on the homes of critics, the unofficial detention centers run by the Revolutionary Guards, and the use of torture to extract confessions. Should Rouhani decide to act resolutely, he might be able to intervene and slow down such systematic abuse.

Rouhani and his allies in the government have argued that they must first secure a nuclear deal with the West, and that such a victory will propel their efforts in other thorny areas, especially citizens' rights. But most activists and democracy seekers of various backgrounds view this position with caution. In Iran, there is always some great, challenging political feat that must be achieved before the regime can get around to moderating itself and protecting its citizens. "First we must gain control of parliament," the reformists used to argue, back in the era of Mohammad Khatami. "First we must unseat Ahmadinejad," they claimed during the disastrous eight years of his tenure. "First we must improve the economy," they say now. And in the meanwhile, years and years have passed; countless Iranians have been executed, imprisoned, and tortured; and thousands of journalists, academics, and activists have been cast into permanent exile.

The same laws govern the lives of those who remained behind. That is why I, and most activists and thinkers who wish to see Iran democratize, have moved beyond the "First this, and then . . ." mode of thinking. Either Iran is led by politicians and reformers who will begin the painful, onerous task of fixing the country from within, brick by brick, law by law, or we will continue to stumble along, the economy deteriorating by the day, the middle class zoning out on Turkish soap operas, while Iran's enormous potential as a regional superpower is frittered away, until it is a second-class state that is shunned by the world and viewed by its neighbors as a pestilence.

The only way Rouhani can find a route to meaningful change, to a real victory over the hard-line ideologues, is by relying on the strength of Iran's disaffected masses. If he allows people to stage public demonstrations, if he permits newspapers to publish more freely, if he lets intellectuals and journalists and community leaders hold public meetings and exchange ideas in open debate, he can create a wave of public support for change that will shake the system to its core and force the traditionalists and the fundamentalists and conservatives—led by the supreme leader at the top—to retreat.

Although Iran's nuclear negotiations tumbled in and out of the news headlines, in a seemingly endless process that defied resolution, by the end of 2014 my thinking about the country's "inalienable" nuclear rights, as the regime liked to call them, had changed. For much of the 2000s, I believed staunchly that international law gave Iran a legitimate right to nuclear power and that the government—despite being undemocratic and extremist in most of its policies—was correct in demanding this right from the international community. Most of the Iranians I knew, especially those living inside the country and enduring the economic deterioration and privation that resulted from the Western sanctions, had once felt the same way.

It was, perhaps, a simple sense of national pride or, for some, nationalism. Iranians understood well that the reason they were growing poorer by the day was that their government wouldn't budge on the issue of uranium enrichment. For the public, it was hard to decide what to think. Since 2007, when the nuclear issue began to seriously undermine Iran's relationship with the world, the government had gagged the domestic media from covering the nuclear program outside of official decrees. There were no op-eds or columns or reported analyses that dispassionately examined, and helped the public understand, how a nuclear program would benefit or undermine Iran's national interests. This gag order essentially prevented the media from fulfilling their proper role, keeping the public informed about an issue of vital national importance. As the sanctions steadily ground down Iranians' quality of life, I realized that I, too, did not know enough. Would it all be worth it, in the end, even if it was our right?

In 2013, at a roundtable in Belfast held by the Nobel Women's Initiative, I met an extraordinary woman named Rebecca Johnson, a renowned expert on nuclear disarmament and nonproliferation. She had visited Iran in the past, and she made some compelling and incisive points about the environmental dangers of nuclear energy and how urgent it was for countries to seek out and pursue renewable energy sources that would not pose the sorts of grave risks to their population that nuclear power does. I invited her to spend some time with me and my colleagues and organized a workshop where she could meet with a number of Iranian human rights and civil-society activists. She brought along some of her colleagues, several of whom were nuclear physicists, and they demystified a number of the arguments the Islamic Republic had upheld to justify why it was pursuing nuclear power so doggedly. We learned that nuclear power was wholly unrelated to the research involved in radiation therapy for cancer, for example, and also about the dangers of toxic waste from nuclear enrichment.

After meeting with Rebecca and her colleagues and

devoting those hours to understanding a subject that was fairly specialized, I came to entirely change my views on nuclear power and Iran's pursuit of its right to a nuclear program. I came to see that nuclear power, even when used for peaceful purposes, is rife with dangers. Germany has reversed its course and will be shutting down all its nuclear power plants by 2022. The United States has refrained from building any new ones. The catastrophe at the Japanese Fukushima plant in 2011 only underscored how perilous nuclear power can be, even when overseen by a diligent and responsible state—which, alas, Iran is not.

If the Islamic Republic is determined to have nuclear power so it can build a bomb, that is reckless and pathological. If it seeks, as it claims, only to produce fuel for its nuclear reactor at Bushehr, then this is not in Iran's interests. Iran is drenched in sunlight and could make fast, effective use of solar energy. It sits atop the world's third largest oil reserves and the second largest reserves of natural gas. In addition, one of the world's most significant earthquake faults lies straight beneath Iran; it regularly produces tremors and, every few years, a major quake. With all of this taken together, it's clear that Iran is not a country that needs to or should gamble with its citizens' lives by pursuing nuclear power. We simply must not.

It was after this shift in my views that I started a campaign aimed at bringing the question of nuclear energy to the center of public debate inside Iran. Iranians needed to hear about the realities of nuclear energy, and to learn precisely what it was that they were sacrificing for, during their many years of financial hardship under sanctions. The campaign slowly gained traction, and with time, people inside Iran found the courage to speak up and carve out a space in which to discuss what was best for the country. In 2014, during a panel discussion at Tehran University, the professor of political science Sadegh Zibakalam sat alongside Ahmad Shirzad, a former MP and current physics professor. They said publicly that the nuclear program had inflicted a greater blow to Iran than eight years of devastating war with Iraq.

In August 2014 a young Iranian mathematician, Maryam Mirzakhani, won the world's top math prize, the Fields Medal, often called "the Nobel Prize of math." Iranians were thrilled and could talk about nothing else on social media, congratulating Maryam and sharing in the pride of her accomplishment. Iranian women pursuing higher education inside the country had suffered acutely under Ahmadinejad, who had instituted gender quotas across numerous disciplines, effectively making it impossible for women to study physics, chemistry, and tens of other subjects at numerous universities. For those struggling to find institutions that permitted them to train in the subjects they loved, their horizons had never looked so limited. Student visas were increasingly difficult to secure, a number of programs teaching English as a second language no longer offered exams in Iran because of sanctions, and the fall in the Iranian *rial*'s value made studying abroad even in less expensive countries like Malaysia impossible.

I sent Maryam a public message of congratulations, to recognize her incredible accomplishment and to remind all those Iranian women inside the country that striving for an education was still worth it. Maryam, after all, had earned her bachelor's degree at Sharif University of Technology before moving to the United States for graduate work. I made a request of Maryam in my message: "When you go back to Tehran, ask why a young physicist is sitting in prison."

This resonated widely in the Iranian media, and it captured neatly why Iran has such a massive brain drain of educated, talented young people. Omid Kokabee, a young Iranian experimental laser physicist, had been arrested and imprisoned in 2011. Before his arrest, Kokabee had been a postdoctoral researcher at the University of Texas; he had returned to Iran to visit his family, whereupon the authorities had sentenced him to ten years in prison for allegedly "cooperating with enemy states." In a 2013 letter written from Evin Prison, however, Kokabee said that his arrest had followed his refusal to cooperate with the authorities on a military research project. Since then, thirty-one Nobel laureates in physics have signed a letter to the Iranian government demanding his release.

Kokabee's experience, together with Maryam's, illustrated why so many of Iran's brightest young students left the country. Abroad they could pursue research work at the world's most prestigious and academically advanced institutions, without fear of butting up against a security state that viewed researchers and scientists with either suspicion or designs of recruitment. As Maryam's extraordinary achievement showed, abroad they could ascend to the greatest heights in their field.

Inside Iran, the climate for women, especially, was deteriorating by the day, despite Rouhani's election. In September 2014, Tehran's chief of police for public places announced that women would no longer be permitted to work in the city's cafés and restaurants, pushing thousands of women, especially university students, out of work. Female musicians reported that cities were increasingly refusing to permit them to perform onstage. Tehran's mayor, Mohammad Baqer Qalibaf, decreed around the same time that women civil servants should not work alongside men, adding that women working long hours outside the home in the company of male colleagues undermined family life. And particularly disappointing for young people, the authorities in the capital even forbade women to watch that year's soccer World Cup, as had long been the custom, in public cinemas and cafés. The moves were all part of a stealthy segregation plan, deployed piecemeal over time in and across different spheres, that threatened to remake public life in Iran and push women, who participated vibrantly despite the state's myriad restrictions, to the margins.

Rouhani's government did seek to intervene. His officials argued that gender restrictions in the workplace, for example, contravened Iran's obligations as a signatory to the International Labour Organization. But the fact was that conservatives had retained enormous clout throughout the system, and their collective influence and determination to reshape Iran to fit their deeply patriarchal, Islamist vision easily outweighed Rouhani's limited will to resist.

The destructive legacy of Ahmadinejad's tenure could be felt in all of these developments. For eight years, he had systematically persecuted the country's civic activists. He had also singlehandedly snuffed out its women's movement and, most dangerously, had renormalized the idea that women should be open targets for the state and ordinary Iranians alike. In the fall of 2014, a spate of serial attacks against women rocked the city of Isfahan. Men on motorbikes threw buckets of sulfuric acid in the faces of women stopped at traffic lights in their cars or walking down the street. Despite the panic spreading among the women of Isfahan as the number of assaults rose to at least fifteen, the police failed to find and arrest the attackers. On Facebook, women in Isfahan discussed the attacks openly and said they were being targeted for what the vigilantes deemed "immodest" dress. Whether the assailants were acting independently or on orders, I cannot say. But what was clear was that the political climate was hospitable to

such violence against women. Hard-liners in parliament were trying to push through a bill that would have
protected vigilantes seeking to "enforce" Islamic law.

When it comes to the most extreme forms of violence against women that we see in the Middle East or
in countries with Muslim majorities, Iran—broadly
speaking, and looking at the level of society itself—has
among the fewest problems. In countries like Pakistan,
for example, acid attacks are an almost daily occur-
rence. In many societies, honor killings, forced marriage, and domestic violence are mainstream realities.
Iran suffers from all of these ills, but with far less severity than many of its neighbors. Iran is not Afghani-
stan, and it is not Egypt or Saudi Arabia. Literacy
among Iranian girls and young women is nearly 99
percent, women make up over 60 percent of all university students, and if you walk the streets of any Iranian city at rush hour, you will see women streaming
out of workplaces, boarding buses and subways alongside men. They are an active, engaged part of public
life, and they increasingly often serve as primary bread-
winners in their households.

I describe all of this to show how much Iranian society itself has evolved. The regime's hard-liners are a
social minority today, and though society itself has
bounded ahead, those representing the extremist minority are, tragically, in control. And like all dictators,
they are clinging to power with vicious violence. The
Iranian government's ambitions in the region, espe-

cially, are kindling fierce resentment among Arabs
from Egypt to Iraq, and I am nervous about what dangers this will pose for Iran. What I hope and pray for
most of all is that the Islamic Republic's present leaders
will not change Iran inalterably. I know that one day I
will go back to Iran. But I am not sure that the Iran I
return to will be the same as the one I left behind.

The same night I sent my congratulations to Maryam
Mirzakhani, the brilliant mathematician, I received a
text message from an unknown number:

> Do you want us to do to her what we did to you?
> If you don't shut up, we'll shut you up.

In December 2014, my colleague Narges Mohammadi (who had served several terms in prison for
clashes with the state) flew to the eastern border city of
Zahedan to bestow a prize from the Defenders of
Human Rights Center on Molavi Abdul-Hamid, the
Sunni Friday prayer leader of the region. Abdul-
Hamid has something approaching rock-star status
among Iran's Sunnis, who are often ethnically Baluch
and hail from that border province. Iran is a Shiite
majority country, and its Sunni citizens, who make up
about 10 percent of the population, face serious discrimination. They are made to feel like second-class
Iranians and are never able to secure senior positions

in government, the military, or any state-affiliated institution. In Tehran, a city of nearly eight million people, the authorities have not permitted the building of
any new Sunni mosques.

With the sectarian tensions in the region rising every
day, it is more imperative than ever for the Iranian
state to embrace its Sunnis, so that Iran remains invul-
nerable to the kind of sect-based violence and insecu-
rity that is ravaging Iraq and Syria and threatens other
parts of the Persian Gulf. Molavi Abdul-Hamid is a
wonderful potential ally in this effort, if only the state
would appreciate him.

Earlier that year, when the Sunni extremist group
Jaish al-Adl attacked an eastern border post on the
Iran-Pakistan boundary line and took five Iranian border guards hostage, it was only Abdul-Hamid's inter-
vention that secured their release. He sent emissaries
to the hostage takers and beseeched them, "Please, for
my sake, release these Iranians." And they did.

He is constantly telling the Baluch to calm down,
soothing their anger, trying to keep them peaceful and
in the fold. He is an asset and an upstanding Iranian
citizen. But the Islamic Republic despises him. The
authorities have imprisoned his sons, killed some of
his relatives, and banned him from traveling. Yet he
continues to work to calm sectarian and ethnic tensions. He does so despite what some MPs stood up and
said about him in parliament, after he secured the release of the border hostages: they claimed that the hos-

tage taking was his fault, on the logic that if the separatists listened to him, then clearly he had instigated the attack in the first place.

The prize the center gave to Abdul-Hamid made a great deal of noise, and I'm glad for this. We are going through such troubled times in the region, and my aim is to bring Iranians of different groups and sects closer together. I want to tell them, "We're with you; you're a part of us. We're all Iranians, together." This kind of sentiment hasn't really emerged properly in Iranian society. While many public intellectuals, writers, and pundits feel this way, and are progressive in their thinking about sect and ethnicity, it hasn't become popular yet to express such ideas openly. If the human rights community can take the lead in this, I think we will help preserve a sense of broad, inclusive Iranian identity that will serve us well, as the Middle East stumbles through a period of heightened sectarianism.

The day after Narges traveled to Zahedan to give Abdul-Hamid the prize, she was summoned for interrogation by the intelligence authorities. Instead of calling him by his name, they referred to the cleric as "Molavi Abdel-Khabees," using a rhyming pun that substituted "malicious" for his last name. They demanded to know why we had given the prize to him.

"Is it illegal to give someone a prize?" Narges asked them. "And at a time of such tensions, is it such a bad thing to bring people closer together?"

It was astonishing that with so much sectarian instability in the region, the Iranian state was not doing more to include its Sunni citizens and project itself in the region as an Islamic power that had the loyalty of both Shia and Sunni Iranians. But as with so many other matters, the Islamic Republic looked only one step ahead, instead of ten.

CHAPTER 20

The Suspicious Neighbor

♦

When the portly Iranian man opened the door of the office next to mine and called out in Persian, "Hello, Mrs. Ebadi!," my first thought was that I would need to move. The office I had rented in London as the base for my human rights NGO, the Centre for Supporters of Human Rights, could not have been in a more inaccessible building. It was a towering modern glass structure in Hammersmith that housed the executive offices of Harrods, and it took security very seriously. The reception desk required ID of anyone entering the building, and the café lounge downstairs was run by the building management itself and admitted only residents and their guests. The place was so expensive that instead of springing for a proper office, I had rented only a tiny room, about the size of a small Persian rug. It fit just two small desks, arranged so close together that when two people used the office at the same time, they bumped elbows constantly.

Various E.U. security officials had suggested that I consider hiring a bodyguard, but I was reluctant to do so. During those years in Iran when the state had assigned me "bodyguards," out of ostensible fear for my safety, it had been a form of intense surveillance. Everywhere I went, the two security agents were my shadow, listening to my conversations, observing my interactions. If Javad and I had dinner with friends in a Tehran restaurant, they sat at the table beside us. Although I knew that in Europe a bodyguard would genuinely be looking after my safety, the thought of someone trailing me at all times made me uncomfortable. I couldn't stand the idea of another person spending the whole day on their feet, standing about looking after me.

Still, I knew I had to be very careful on my own. Iranian intelligence agents were energetically active in Europe; a number of exiled Iranian dissidents and journalists had had their laptops stolen in mysterious thefts in which the burglar took nothing else of value, and London's universities were a favorite finishing school for young Islamic Republic spies. So rather than a bodyguard, I preferred to live and work in highly secure buildings. Because I traveled so much, a small office posed no problems, and I had imagined that this glass building in Hammersmith, where nearly everyone was British and went about in formal business attire, would be suitable.

Until the day a mysterious Iranian man turned up in the office directly next to mine and introduced himself as my new neighbor. My assistant, Leila, and I were astonished, and we greeted him cautiously.

"I know we've met before in Tehran. Was it at Mrs. Kar's office?" He was in his mid-forties, with red cheeks, thick black hair, and arched eyebrows.

"Were you one of her clients?"

"No, no—I was just there to talk to her about a writer we both knew."

"I'm afraid I don't recall meeting you at all."

He explained that he was in the petrochemicals business, had rented the office three months ago, and had finally gotten around to moving in today. He offered me his card. I asked how he managed to do petrochemical trading out of Europe, given the international banking sanctions against Iran.

"We know how to get around those," he said, laughing. "We work with the Russians."

I politely told him I had a phone call to make, and Leila and I went into our office. His card bore a company logo, and one side was written entirely in Cyrillic and included a Russian address. I scrawled "suspicious neighbor" on it and pulled out my notebook to work.

A few minutes later, there was a knock at the door.

"Do you mind if I take up a few minutes of your time?" he asked.

We made space for him in the awkward little room, and those few minutes turned into an hour and a half. He started with "What are you doing here in London?"

and continued with endless questions: about what my dealings with Iran currently were, where I received my funding, who I worked with. It reminded me of a Tehran interrogation session, the kind I had endured so many times in my life. How intrepid they were, I thought, to have reenacted history here in the heart of London, renting an office next door to mine, just as they had done in Tehran.

We talked about a number of things, but I made the point again that although the Iranian government viewed me with great suspicion as some kind of political alternative to the current regime, I hadn't the slightest desire for political power. I knew the authorities didn't believe it, and that the man sitting beside me probably did not, either.

But, I still wonder, do they think I am so stupid as to really wish to become the president of Iran? At such a tumultuous moment in history, with the Middle East festering with open conflict, and Iran a country teeming with prisoners and political opposition of seventy stripes? I sometimes wonder what kind of person they take me for. Perhaps they themselves are so addicted to power and privilege that they imagine others must be seeking the same. They ask me so repeatedly where I receive my funding, while they know—their files document—that I have never been corrupt, and the way I live my life has shown that. If it were any different, my office might have been larger than a rug, and I wouldn't be living in a modest apartment, riding the red double-decker buses of London.

I could have easily brushed this man off, but I deliberately answered everything he asked me. I wanted to prove yet another time to the intelligence officials of the Islamic Republic—if indeed he was one, which seemed likely—that I had nothing to hide. That I worked in human rights, that my work was legal, and that I did not contravene Iranian law in the process and had never done so. I told him about the activities the Centre for Supporters of Human Rights was now actively pursuing, promoting research and understanding around the compatibility of Islam and an egalitarian legal framework for women, particularly in the realm of family law.

The conversation jumped about, soon moving to Iran's economy. He mentioned the billionaire Babak Zanjani, who stands accused of corruption.

"Zanjani hasn't done anything wrong. It was suggested to me that I go and sell some oil, but I said no," he told me. "But I could have become as wealthy as him."

I remained silent, and didn't say that in my view Babak Zanjani was an outrageous thief.

"I'm afraid we won't be neighbors for long," I said. "We're moving out in January."

"Oh, where are you going?"

"We're moving to the United Nations in New York. They sometimes have space for NGOs and have promised us an office." This wasn't exactly true, but I wanted to convey the sense that we had protectors in the world.

Let him chase me there, I thought. When he was finished, he thanked me and left, and I imagined I would see him again, or at least an assistant; someone would surely be using the expensive office he had rented. When I told my colleagues and friends about the suspicious neighbor, they all agreed that he was certainly an intelligence agent.

"They sent him to either kill you or talk with you. The first is unlikely, as they wouldn't have bothered to rent an office first," said a friend drily. "But they are still scared of you, to be watching this closely."

Sometimes I look at his card, which remains in my drawer. The international agents of the Islamic Republic all have multiple identities and passports. Even the most notorious officials, the hanging judges associated with the worst human rights abuses and the officials close to the nuclear program who are on the European Union's list of sanctioned officials prohibited from traveling to the West, have alternative passports. These authentic documents are produced by the state but show different identities, enabling these men to travel despite sanctions. Names don't matter. They use their third and fourth passports and fly to London or Paris, laughing at all of us.

Months have passed and the office sits empty, the lights off and the little glass window that looks out onto the corridor blocked from the inside with a piece of cardboard. I think about the listening equipment that must be inside and wonder whether it has gathered dust.

♦ ♦ ♦

Most evenings when I am in London, I stand outside on my small balcony and look out across the Thames at the city spread before me. I am accustomed to gazing at mountains, and the outline of the Alborz is still etched in my mind, but I try to remind myself that I am not the first Iranian who has lost her country because of speaking truth to power. Since Persian poets first began committing verse to paper, we have been able to trace our country's long struggle for justice through literature, and perhaps this is why Iranians take such solace in satire. One evening in London, the great Iranian satirist Hadi Khorsandi staged a play, in Persian, called *The Trial of Shirin Ebadi's Sister*. Although it was bittersweet to watch, sitting there in the darkened theater, I thanked God that I was alive to see the worst days of my life turned to art.

Khorsandi himself played the clerical judge; he sat behind a desk wearing flip-flops under his robes, which he rearranged importantly. His mobile rang with the news that the police were bringing Shirin Ebadi's sister into his court for trial.

A woman walked onto the stage, and the judge immediately flayed her with questions, many utterly stupid. Every time she tried to interject, he shouted at her, "Be quiet, or I'll execute you!" Though it was an interrogation, the judge posed and answered his own questions, as the woman grew more agitated.

"So, have you ever been to Shirin Ebadi's house? What was she doing? Was she making koofteh [meatballs]? I bet she had one hand in the koofteh and was speaking to the CIA with the other!"

"Hajj Agha, you can't make koofteh with one hand."

"Silence! I'll execute you!"

After more such questioning, the muezzin's call to pray sounded. The judge excused himself.

"Let me go have lunch and pray; then we'll execute you after."

After he exited the stage, the woman faced the audience and answered her own mobile phone. "This idiot thinks I'm Shirin Ebadi's sister and won't leave me alone! They told me that he wasn't feeling well and asked me to come down, but he won't let me get a word in to explain."

At this point, the audience realizes that she is a nurse employed by the judiciary.

When the judge returns to the courtroom, she bursts out before he has a chance to speak: "Please, just listen for one second. I'm here to take your blood pressure!"

And the story ends like this, a satire of justice in the Iranian court system. Khorsandi said he was inspired by something I said in the wake of my sister's arrest: "When they do this to a sister of a Nobel laureate, imagine what they do to a nameless student or a journalist without a reputation."

The play, I hope and pray, will only be a footnote in my story. I still believe that one day I will live again in the same city as my sister and brother, and wake up to the birds and the honking and the shouts of the metal scrap vendor that tell me I am in Tehran. The orchard remains in the care of my friends; by now the trees must be a foot taller, and I imagine that one day I will again taste their fruit and sit under their shade, recalling the days when Javad and I planted them with such care. I have lost more than I ever thought possible, but I nevertheless thank God that even from exile I can still work to build my country. It is for the sake of Iran and its people, its potential and its greatness, that I have taken each and every step along this journey. And I know that one day Iranians will find their own path to the freedom and justice they deserve.

My dear friend the great poet Simin Behbahani died in Tehran while I was in London. I could not attend her funeral to say goodbye, but I thought of our long walks together in the Alborz foothills. I remembered our talks about the fragility of life and everything that bound us to Iran. Has ever a country been so loved? As I go about my second life, her verses often echo in my mind.

> My country, I shall build you again,
> even if with bricks of my life.
> I shall erect pillars beneath your roof,
> even if with my own bones.
> I shall again smell those flowers
> favored by your young,
> I shall again cleanse you of blood
> with the flood of my tears.

◆

In the summer of 2015, just as I was finishing this
memoir, after two years of intensive negotiations and
many more of open conflict, Iran signed a historic nuclear agreement with the West. For once in the long,
fraught history of Iran-U.S. relations, both countries
were led by moderates keen to move beyond the legacy
of mistrust and to accommodate each other's concerns.
President Barack Obama sought to assure Americans
that the accord he was striking with Iran would put in
place limits on Iran's nuclear program that for years
had eluded the international community: a cap on uranium enrichment and the number of operable centrifuges, as well as an inspections regime that would
ensure transparency and assure the West that Iran could
not seek a breakout capability for a nuclear weapon.
President Hassan Rouhani, for his part, succeeded in

fulfilling the mandate on which he was elected by the Iranian people: negotiating an end to the sanctions that were strangling Iran's economy while maintaining the essentials of a peaceful nuclear program, to which Iran was entitled under the Nuclear Nonproliferation Treaty.

For ordinary Iranians inside the country, who have lived for the past decade under the threat of a potential American or Israeli military attack, and who have suffered the devastating impact of sanctions, the deal is cause for great hope. Iran's currency, the *rial,* has steadily dropped in value in recent years, as the country lost its ability to trade with the world and export its oil. More than anything, Iranians want their economy to improve and their nation to emerge from political isolation. They want their government to spend whatever funds it does gain access to on Iranians inside the country, rather than on weapons for Hezbollah in Lebanon or Bashar al-Assad's troops in Syria.

Within days after the negotiators sealed the deal, Britain reopened its embassy in Tehran, and European and American companies rushed to Tehran to ready themselves for the economic boom that is expected once banking sanctions are lifted. As history has proven, countries that interact with the world, forge commercial ties, and can elicit foreign investment develop stakes in being integrated with the global community. Having such stakes can, with time, potentially change the behavior of Iran's government. President Rouhani, Foreign Minister Javad Zarif, and the other moderates who support the nuclear deal believe it is the only way to advance the country's national interest. Their interpretation of national interest is centered on economic growth and a stable relationship with the region and the world. But there are hard-liners in Iran who cling to the ideal of uranium enrichment at any cost; their vision of national interest is interlaced with ideology. It remains to be seen whose vision will prevail, and whether this deal, which many deem so historic, will fundamentally alter the Islamic Republic's troubled trajectory in the world.

As I write this, the nuclear deal has passed through both the U.S. Congress and Iran's parliament, and what is essentially an arms control treaty will soon be ratified. But the real problem still remains. Iran continues to interfere in the neighboring countries of the Middle East. Iran, as the only country with an overwhelming Shia majority, seeks to assert itself as the leading Shia power in the world, to cultivate Shias in other countries, and to encourage them to rise up against their rulers. This ambition underpins Iran's involvement in Lebanon, Iraq, and more recently Yemen. Naturally, Iran's behavior has deeply alarmed Saudi Arabia, which sees itself as the Sunni opposing pole in the region, and the two countries' rivalry is today destabilizing the region in ways that will doubtless continue, despite the signing of the nuclear accord.

Iran's supreme leader, Ayatollah Ali Khamenei, has declared several times since the agreement was signed that the Islamic Republic still does not trust the United

States, and that America remains the enemy. For Iran's clerics, America's enmity has been the bedrock upon which the revolution was built; they invoke America's nefarious intentions each time they wish to suppress the country's native opposition, claiming dissidents are working at Washington's behest. It is hard to imagine an Islamic Republic that is at peace with the United States, for a revolution not perpetually at war with its enemies becomes duty bound to be accountable to its citizens. This is something to which Iran's rulers have shown themselves to be averse.

At a moment when so many Iranians are celebrating the end to their country's worst period in recent memory, I do not wish to appear the sour cynic. But those of us with long experience of this government know it too intimately to imagine that everything brutal and illiberal about the Islamic Republic will transform overnight. It is too early to judge what the nuclear deal will mean for Iran, the Middle East, and, indeed, the world. Like all my countrypeople, I will watch and wait eagerly, hoping for a path that opens up, ultimately, onto freedom.

AUTHOR'S NOTE

◆

My aim in writing this book is to bear witness to what the people of Iran have endured in the past decade. By reading it, you will see how a police state can affect people's lives and throw families into disarray. What you can take away from my personal story is this: if a government can behave in this way with a Nobel Peace laureate who has access to the platform of world media, and who is herself a lawyer with intimate knowledge of the country's legal system, you can imagine what it does to ordinary Iranians, who have no such means or expertise at their disposal. I am compelled to share my story on behalf of the many faceless Iranians, political prisoners and prisoners of conscience, who sit today in the prisons of Iran, an Iran that has become one of the world's largest prisons for journalists, lawyers, women's rights activists, and students, who instead of

studying are languishing in cellblocks, yet another generation whose talent and dreams are squandered. But
the hardship imposed by the Iranian police state has
not caused the people of Iran to lose their hope for
change or their willingness to reach for it.

ACKNOWLEDGMENTS

♦

There are many people to whom I owe my thanks, both
now and over the years.

I'm grateful to my longtime friend Abdolkarim La-
hiji, from whom I've learned so many things. My
daughters, Negar and Nargess, who were my champi-
ons throughout the difficult period following 2009
and who have always warmed my heart. My former husband, Javad, for enduring more than thirty-seven years
of hardship as a result of my work. I thank him, truly,
for his forbearance, and wish him happiness in the
new life he has started.

My brother, Jafar, and my sister, Nooshin, for their
continued support; I am truly sorry that because of my
work they have had to endure so many interrogations at
the hands of security officials.

My wonderful colleagues Abdolfatah Soltani and

Mohammad Seifzadeh, and Narges Mohammadi, who all worked so closely with me to found the Defenders of Human Rights Center and who, for this reason, sit in prison today. It is only with their help, and the efforts of so many other colleagues, that we were able to make such strides in human rights in Iran in such a relatively short span of time. Thanks as well to all the rest of my colleagues at the center, whose hard work and efforts have helped ease the difficulties of exile. I hope that one day we can gather together in a democratic, secular Iran and work to defend the human rights of those who are victimized.

The Nobel women laureates with whom I formed the Nobel Women's Initiative, and the group's staff, all of whom have been a steadfast source of support.

Azadeh Moaveni, without whose efforts, day and night, I would not have had the opportunity to publish this book. David Ebershoff, for his dedication in reading these pages with such acuity and for his invaluable advice. Karolina Sutton, for putting her long-standing experience at my disposal and for helping me clear the various obstacles that stood in the way.